KEYBOARD CHORD SONG BOOK

S Club 7 Great Hits

Best Friend 6

Bring It All Back 10

Bring The House Down 3

The Colour Of Blue 14

Cross My Heart 20

Friday Night 17

I Really Miss You 26

I'll Keep Waiting 23

It's A Feel Good Thing 29

Natural 40

Reach 32

S Club Party 36

Two In A Million 46

You're My Number One 43

GW00643623

This publication is not authorised for sale in the
United States of America and/or Canada.

London/New York/Sydney/Madrid/Tokyo

Exclusive distributors:
Music Sales Limited
8/9 Frith Street,
London W1D 3JB, England.
Music Sales Pty Limited
120 Rothschild Avenue
Rosebery, NSW 2018,
Australia.

Order No.AM962852
ISBN 0-7119-8046-2
This book © Copyright 2000 by Wise Publications

Book design by Chloë Alexander
Music arranged & engraved by Roger Day
Compiled by Nick Crispin

Cover photograph courtesy of London Features International.
Inside photographs courtesy of All Action, Redferns and
London Features International.

Printed in the United Kingdom by
Printwise (Haverhill) Limited, Suffolk.

Your Guarantee of Quality
As publishers, we strive to produce every book to the highest
commercial standards. The music has been freshly engraved and
the book has been carefully designed to minimise awkward page
turns and to make playing from it a real pleasure. Particular care
has been given to specifying acid-free, neutral-sized paper made
from pulps which have not been elemental chlorine bleached. This
pulp is from farmed sustainable forests and was produced with
special regard for the environment. Throughout, the printing and
binding have been planned to ensure a sturdy, attractive
publication which should give years of enjoyment. If your copy
fails to meet our high standards, please inform us and we will
gladly replace it.

Music Sales' complete catalogue describes thousands of titles and
is available in full colour sections by subject, direct from Music
Sales Limited. Please state your areas of interest and send a
cheque/postal order for £1.50 for postage to: Music Sales Limited,
Newmarket Road, Bury St. Edmunds, Suffolk IP33 3YB.

www.musicsales.com

Bring The House Down

Words & Music by Andy Watkins, Paul Wilson & Tracy Ackerman

Intro

|N.C. |N.C. |N.C. |N.C. |E |A/E |

|E |A/E |E |D/E |E |D |

Verse 1

    E   D/E
As the night draws in, let the game begin,
   A/E E A/E E D/E| E |
It's a groove thing.
         E   D/E
Let your feet decide, gonna catch a ride,
   A/E E A/E E   D/E| E |
Keep on mov - - in'.
            C#m7
So let's go away,
    F#m   C#m7
The mood can't be that hard to reach.
    F#m   Gmaj7
The night will just take us there.

Bridge 1

      E
And all you gotta do is...

All you gotta do is

Chorus 1

         E
Bring the house down,
D/E   E
Raise the roof and get on the floor.
A/E   E   D   E
(House down, raise the roof, get on the floor.)

E
Let's bring the house down,

D/E   **E**
Really want to hear you shouting more, more, more.

 D   **E**
(Really want to hear some more.)

Verse 2

        E   **D/E**
You stay in bed with a sleepy head

   A/E **E A/E E**   **D/E**| **E**|
Doing no - - thing.

            E   **D/E**
You can always try just to walk on but

   A/E E   **A/E E**   **D/E**| **E**|
It will pull you in.

             C#m7
We're flying away,

    F#m   **C#m7**
We fall into this fantasy

             F#m   **Gmaj7**
Where the groove will carry us on.

Bridge 2

     E
And all we gotta do is…

All we gotta do is

Chorus 2

       E
Bring the house down,

D/E   **E**
Raise the roof and get on the floor.

 A/E   **E**   **D**   **E**
(House down, raise the roof, get on the floor.)

          E
Let's bring the house down,

D/E   **E**
Really want to hear you shouting more, more, more.

 D   **E**
(Really want to hear some more.)

Middle

D
Everybody do your thing,

                 E
Let's bring the house down.

D
Everybody spread your wings,

                 E
Let's bring the house down.

Verse 3

          C#m7
So let's go away,

    F#m   **C#m7**
The mood can't be that hard to reach.

    F#m   **Gmaj7**
The night will just take us there.

Bridge 3

     E
And all you gotta do is…

All you gotta do is

Chorus 3

‖:   **E**
  Bring the house down,

D/E   **E**
Raise the roof and get on the floor.

 A/E **E**   **D**   **E**
(House down, raise the roof, get on the floor.)

               E
Let's bring the house down,

D/E   **E**
Really want to hear you shouting more, more, more.

  D   **E**   :‖ *Repeat to fade*
(Really want to hear some more.)

Best Friend

Words & Music by Timothy Laws, Stephen Emanuel & Bradley McIntosh

E♭

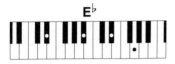

Fm

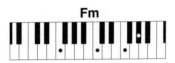

B♭m7

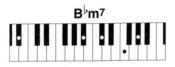

Cm7

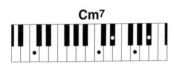

Intro

N.C.
Come on, come on, best friend.

| E♭ Fm   B♭m7 | B♭m7 Cm7 | E♭ Fm   B♭m7 | B♭m7 Cm7 |

               E♭ Fm   B♭m7   Cm7
We all need a best friend,   a best friend.

| E♭ Fm   B♭m7 | B♭m7 Cm7 |

Verse 1

E♭ Fm
    I remember when we was young

          B♭m7   **Cm7**
Playing pool after school, keeping it cool.

         E♭   **Fm**
People say we were the troublesome two.

         B♭m7   **Cm7**
I know the girls liked me and you,

E♭ Fm   **B♭m7**
    I can never forget the times you've covered my back.

            Cm7
You helped me out and cut me some slack.

           E♭   **Fm**
There was nothing you would never do,

    B♭m7   **Cm7**
It's all about me and you.

Bridge 1

             E♭ Fm B♭m7   **Cm7**
You're my bro-ther,   you're my sister,

               E♭   **Fm**
We'll stick together

     B♭m7   **Cm7**
No matter what, no matter what.

Chorus 1

E♭ Fm   B♭m7
Best friend, never gonna let you down.

                       Cm7
Best friend, always gonna be around.

E♭   Fm   B♭m7
You know,   whatever life puts you through

                     Cm7
I'll be there for you.

             E♭ Fm   B♭m7
We all need a best   friend to understand,

            Cm7
A best friend   to take your hand,

        E♭ Fm   B♭m7
You know whatever life puts you through

                     Cm7
I'll be there for you.

Verse 2

E♭   Fm
   You remember the days

                B♭m7   Cm7
When we would kick back,   lay back,

        E♭   Fm
We'd be chilling with the ladies.

     B♭m7   Cm7
Those times were the greatest.

E♭   Fm   B♭m7
  So don't worry about a thing, my friend,

                Cm7
Cos you can count on me, thick or thin.

E♭   Fm
  Cos I'll be there right till the end,

B♭m7   Cm7
Till the end.

Bridge 2

As Bridge 1

Chorus 2

E♭   Fm   B♭m7
Best friend, never gonna let you down.

               Cm7
Best friend, always gonna be around.

    E♭   Fm   B♭m7
You know,   whatever life puts you through

             Cm7
I'll be there for you.

       E♭   Fm   B♭m7
We all need a best   friend to understand,

     Cm7
A best friend   to take your hand,

    E♭   Fm   B♭m7
You know whatever life puts you through

            Cm7
I'll be there for you.

Middle

E♭   Fm   B♭m7   Cm7
  Come on, come on, best friend.

E♭   Fm   B♭m7   Cm7
  Come on, come on, best friend.

E♭   Fm   B♭m7   Cm7
  Come on, come on, best friend.

E♭   Fm   B♭m7   Cm7
  Come on, come on, best friend.

Bridge 3

         E♭   Fm   B♭m7   Cm7
You're my bro-ther,   you're my sister,

          E♭   Fm
We'll stick together

   B♭m7   Cm7
No matter what, no matter what.

Bridge 4

Repeat Bridge 3

Chorus 3

‖:   E♭   Fm   B♭m7
  Best friend, never gonna let you down.

              Cm7
Best friend, always gonna be around.

    E♭   Fm   B♭m7
You know,   whatever life puts you through

             Cm7
I'll be there for you.

         E♭   Fm   B♭m7
We all need a best   friend to understand,

      Cm7
A best friend   to take your hand,

    E♭ Fm   B♭m7
You know whatever life puts you through

           Cm7   :‖ *Repeat to fade*
I'll be there for you.

Bring It All Back

Words & Music by Eliot Kennedy, Mike Percy, Tim Lever & S Club 7

E

Amaj⁷

B

F♯m

A/E

Bsus⁴

F♯m⁷

A

B⁷sus²

Intro

|E   Amaj⁷ |B   F♯m   A/E |E Bsus⁴ F♯m⁷ |

A B⁷sus² E
          (Bring it all back now.)
E   Amaj⁷
Don't stop, never give up.
  B   F♯m   A/E
Hold your head high and reach the top.
     E   Bsus⁴   F♯m⁷
Let the world see what you have got,
    A   B⁷sus² E
Bring it all back to you.

Verse 1

      E   A
Hold on to what you try to be,
      E   A
Your individuality.
        E   A
When the world is on your shoulders
      E   A
Just smile and let it go.
    E   A
If people try to put you down
    E   A
Just walk on by, don't turn around.
    E   A   E   A
You only have to answer to yourself.

Bridge 1

                        B
Don't you know it's true what they say,
   C♯m⁷
In life it ain't easy,

Dmaj7   **B7sus4**

But your time's coming around,

So don't you stop trying.

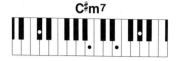

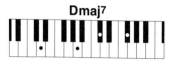

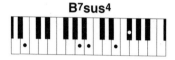

Chorus 1

E   **Amaj7**
Don't stop, never give up,

   B   **F#m**   **A/E**
Hold your head high and reach the top.

    E   **Bsus4**   **F#m7**
Let the world see what you have got,

  A   **B7sus2** **E**
Bring it all back to you.

E   **Amaj7**
Dream of falling in love,

   B   **F#m**   **A/E**
Anything you've been thinking of.

    E   **Bsus4**   **F#m7**
When the world seems to get too tough,

  A   **B7sus2** **E**
Bring it all back to you.

Link

E   **A**
Na na na na na na na na na

E   **A**
Na na na na na.

E   **A**   **E**   **A**
Na na na na na na na na.

Verse 2

     E   **A**
Try not to worry 'bout a thing,

    E   **A**
Enjoy the good times life can bring.

E   **A**
Keep it all beside you,

    E   **A**
Gotta let the feeling show.

more chords overleaf...

```
     E           A
Imagination is the key
       E                   A
Cos you are your own destiny.
E                      A
You never should be lonely
        E                  A
When time is on your side.
```

Bridge 2

```
                        B
Don't you know it's true what they say,
C#m7
Things are sent to try you.
      Dmaj7                 B7sus4
But your time's coming around,
```

So don't you stop trying.

Chorus 2

As Chorus 1

Link

```
‖: E        A
   Na na na na na na na na na
E        A
Na na na na na.
E        A              E     A  :‖
Na na na na na na na na.
```

Bridge 3

```
                        B
Don't you know it's true what they say,
       C#m7
Things happen for a reason.
      Dmaj7                 B7sus4
But your time's coming around,
```

So don't you stop trying.

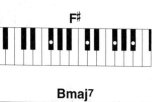
F#

Chorus 3

N.C.
Don't stop, never give up,

Hold your head high and reach the top.

Let the world see what you have got,

Bring it all back to you.

E   **Amaj7**
Dream of falling in love,

 B   **F#m**   **A/E**
Anything you've been thinking of.

   E   **Bsus4**   **F#m7**
When the world seems to get too tough,

   A   **B7sus2** **E**
Bring it all back to you.

Chorus 4

‖: **F#**   **Bmaj7**
  Don't stop, never give up,

  C#   **G#m**   **B/F#**
Hold your head high and reach the top.

 F#   **C#sus4** **G#m7**
Let the world see what you have got,

  B   **C#7sus2 F#**
Bring it all back to you.

F#   **Bmaj7**
Dream of falling in love,

  C#   **G#m**   **B/F#**
Anything you've been thinking of.

  F#   **C#sus4** **G#m7**
When the world seems to get too tough,

  B   **C#7sus2 F#**   :‖ *Repeat ad lib. to fade*
Bring it all back to you.

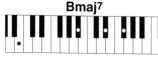
Bmaj7

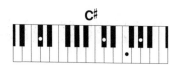
C#

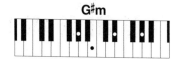
G#m

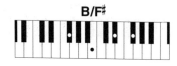
B/F#

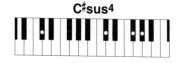
C#sus4

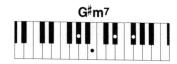
G#m7

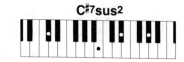
C#7sus2

13

The Colour Of Blue

Words & Music by Lars Aass & Bottolf Løodemel

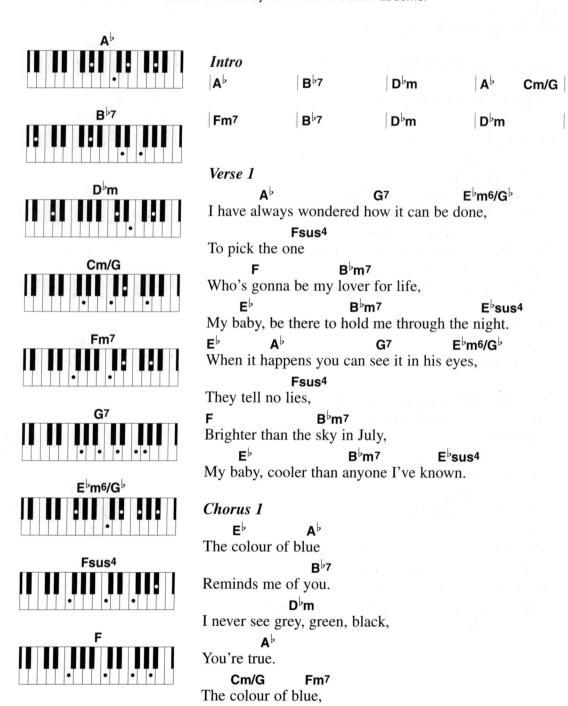

Intro

| A♭ | | B♭7 | | D♭m | | A♭ | Cm/G |

| Fm7 | | B♭7 | | D♭m | | D♭m | |

Verse 1

A♭   G7   E♭m6/G♭
I have always wondered how it can be done,
      Fsus4
To pick the one
      F   B♭m7
Who's gonna be my lover for life,
    E♭   B♭m7   E♭sus4
My baby, be there to hold me through the night.
E♭   A♭   G7   E♭m6/G♭
When it happens you can see it in his eyes,
      Fsus4
They tell no lies,
F   B♭m7
Brighter than the sky in July,
    E♭   B♭m7   E♭sus4
My baby, cooler than anyone I've known.

Chorus 1

    E♭   A♭
The colour of blue
       B♭7
Reminds me of you.
      D♭m
I never see grey, green, black,
      A♭
You're true.
    Cm/G   Fm7
The colour of blue,

       B♭7
No other will do.

     D♭m
In my heart

 E6   **G♭6**   **A♭**
I only feel the colour of blue.

Verse 2

     A♭   **G7**   **E♭m6/G♭**
I say, if you ever felt the way I do,

          Fsus4
Then lucky you,

  F   **B♭m7**   **E♭**
So never go for less than a perfect thing.

         B♭m7   **E♭sus4**
Seek and then hopefully you'll find.

E♭   **A♭**   **G7**   **E♭m6/G♭**
There's a rhythm and a rhyme, you've gotta find it,

        Fsus4
Then you'll see,

  F   **B♭m7**   **E♭**
Cos baby we can go on all night just dancing,

     B♭m7   **E♭sus4**
Doin' it till the break of dawn.

Chorus 2

   E♭   **A♭**
The colour of blue

        B♭7
Reminds me of you.

      D♭m
I never see grey, green, black,

   A♭
You're true.

  Cm/G   **Fm7**
The colour of blue,

      B♭7
No other will do.

    D♭m
In my heart

 E6   **G♭6**   **A♭**
I only feel the colour of blue.

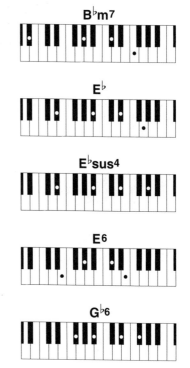

B♭m7 · E♭ · E♭sus4 · E6 · G♭6

Middle

A♭   B♭7 D♭m   A♭   Cm/G
In the rainbow I can see colours of misbelief.

Fm7   B♭7   D♭m E6 G♭6 A♭
There is only one for me and it will forever be.

Instrumental

A♭	B♭7	D♭m	A♭ Cm/G

Fm7	B♭7	D♭m	E6 G♭6

Chorus 3

‖:   A♭
The colour of blue

       B♭7
Reminds me of you.

    D♭m
I never see grey, green, black,

    A♭
You're true.

  Cm/G   Fm7
The colour of blue,

      B♭7
No other will do.

    D♭m
In my heart

 E6   G♭6   A♭ :‖ *Repeat to fade*
I only feel (the colour of blue.)

Friday Night

Words & Music by Tim Laws & Stephen Emanuel

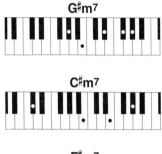

Intro

 N.C.　　　　| G#m7　　　　||

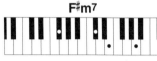

Chorus 1

C#m7　　　　　　　F#m7　A B
　Help us get this started,

C#m7　　　　　F#m7　A B
　Everyone's excited.

C#m7　　　　　　　　　F#m7　　A B
　We'll spend the whole time groovin'

　　A　　　　　　　　G#7　　　　　G#7/B#
Cos what we really like is to party on Friday night.

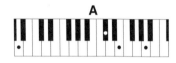

Verse 1

C#m7
　I got my friends and we're here to groove,

F#m7　　　G#m7
Na na na na na.

C#m7
　Nothin's wrong, ain't nothin' to prove,

F#m7　　A B
Na na na na na.

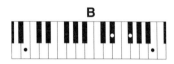

　　　C#m7
Don't need no cash just bring a friend,

F#m7　　　G#m7
Na na na na na.

　　　　C#m7
Cos we're gonna party all night again,

F#m7　　A B
Na na na na na.

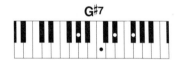

more chords overleaf…

Amaj⁷

Bridge 1

F♯m⁷
One can make a party,

G♯m⁷
Two is not enough to get down,

C♯m⁷
Three, you still get lonely cos tonight's the night for crowds.

F♯m⁷
You can make it better,

G♯m⁷
We can help a little bit too,

Amaj⁷   **G♯7**   **G♯7/B♯**
Us and you together, there ain't nothing we can't do.

Chorus 2

C♯m⁷   **F♯m⁷**   **A**   **B**   **C♯m⁷**
  Help us get this started, cos it's time to call your friends.

      F♯m⁷   **A**   **B**   **C♯m⁷**
Everyone's excited, cos it's Friday night again.

        F♯m⁷   **A**   **B**
We'll spend the whole time groovin' just like we do.

    A   **G♯7**   **G♯7/B♯**
Cos what we really like is to party on Friday night.

Verse 2

C♯m⁷
  School's out now it's time to play,

F♯m⁷   **G♯m⁷**
Na na na na na.

    C♯m⁷
Weekends come like a holiday,

F♯m⁷   **A B**
Na na na na na.

    C♯m⁷
Best thing is now I got my crew,

F♯m⁷   **G♯m⁷**
Na na na na na.

    C♯m⁷
And if you want you can join us too,

F♯m⁷   **A B**
Na na na na na.

Bridge 2

F♯m⁷
One can make a party,

G♯m⁷
Two is not enough to get down,

C♯m⁷
Three, you still get lonely cos tonight's the night for crowds.

F♯m⁷
You can make it better,

G♯m⁷
We can help a little bit too,

Amaj⁷   **G♯7**   **G♯7/B♯**
Us and you together, there ain't nothing we can't do.

Chorus 3

C♯m⁷   **F♯m⁷**   **A**   **B**   **C♯m⁷**
  Help us get this started, cos it's time to call your friends.

                    F♯m⁷   **A**   **B**   **C♯m⁷**
Everyone's excited, cos it's Friday night again.

                         F♯m⁷   **A**   **B**
We'll spend the whole time groovin' just like we do.

        A   **G♯7**   **G♯7/B♯**
Cos what we really like is to party on Friday night.

Middle

‖: **C♯m⁷**
   Monday, Tuesday, come and go.

F♯m⁷   **G♯m⁷**
Wednesday, Thursday, sometimes   slow.

C♯m⁷
  Friday comes just like a dream,

      F♯m⁷   **A**   **B**   :‖
We'll party until it's time to leave.

Bridge 3

As Bridge 2

Chorus 4 *(Repeat to fade)*

As Chorus 3

Cross My Heart

Words & Music by Andy Watkins, Paul Wilson & Tracy Ackerman

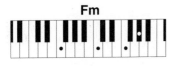

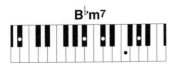

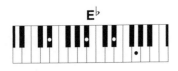

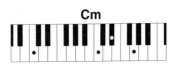

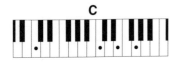

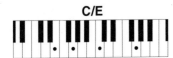

Intro

Fm B♭m7   E♭ Cm Fm   B♭m7 |E♭ C |
Cross__ my heart,   oh. (We said.)

Fm B♭m7   E♭ Cm Fm B♭m7 |E♭ C |
Cross__ my heart,   oh. (I'll be.)

Verse 1

Fm B♭m7 E♭   Cm
  We got it all and we'd be fools to let it go,

Fm   B♭m7   E♭   C
  Cos I need you more and more.

          Fm   B♭m7   E♭   Cm
You're my life and I live for your love that you give,

         Fm   B♭m7   E♭   C
And although my journey's long, I'll soon be home.

B♭m7   E♭   C   B♭m7
Oh,__ it's gonna be so hard on my own.

         E♭   C/E
Oh,__ but I won't be alone.

Chorus 1

Fm   B♭m7
Cross my heart and tell no lies,

E♭   C
No one's leaving you behind,

Fm   B♭m7   E♭ C
Just because we said goodbye,   baby.

Fm   B♭m7
Cross my heart I do believe,

E♭   C
In my thoughts and in my dreams,

Fm   B♭m7   E♭ C
I'll be taking you with me,   baby.

D♭maj7

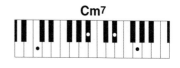

Cm7

Verse 2

Fm   B♭m7   E♭   Cm
  Sometimes I think that I can feel you breathin' on me,

Fm   B♭m7   E♭ C
  You're there, so deep inside.

    Fm   B♭m7   E♭ Cm
And I like what I feel although it's not always real,

   Fm   B♭m7 E♭   C
It helps me carry on till I come home.

B♭m7   E♭   C   B♭m7
Oh,__ it's gonna be so hard on my own.

    E♭   C/E
Oh,__ but I won't be alone.

Chorus 2

Fm   B♭m7
Cross my heart and tell no lies,

E♭   C
No one's leaving you behind,

Fm   B♭m7   E♭ C
Just because we said goodbye,   baby.

Fm   B♭m7
Cross my heart I do believe,

E♭   C
In my thoughts and in my dreams,

Fm B♭m7   E♭ C
I'll be taking you with me,   baby.

Middle

D♭maj7   Cm7
Dream a dream, a dream, a dream, a dreamin'

Cm7   B♭m7
  Whenever you are, you're near me.

D♭maj7   Cm7
Please believe, believe, believe, believe in

C   Fm
  Whatever I say. (I cross my heart.)

Chorus 3

Fm   B♭m7
Cross my heart and tell no lies,

E♭   C
No one's leaving you behind,

Fm   B♭m7   E♭ C
Just because we said goodbye, baby.

Fm   B♭m7
Cross my heart I do believe,

E♭   C
In my thoughts and in my dreams,

Fm   B♭m7   E♭ C
I'll be taking you with me, baby. .

Chorus 4

‖: Fm   B♭m7
 Cross my heart and tell no lies,

E♭   C
No one's leaving you behind,

Fm   B♭m7   E♭ C
Just because we said goodbye, baby.

Fm   B♭m7
Cross my heart I do believe,

E♭   C
In my thoughts and in my dreams,

Fm   B♭m7   E♭ C   :‖ *Repeat to fade*
I'll be taking you with me, baby.

I'll Keep Waiting

Words & Music by Cathy Dennis & Simon Ellis

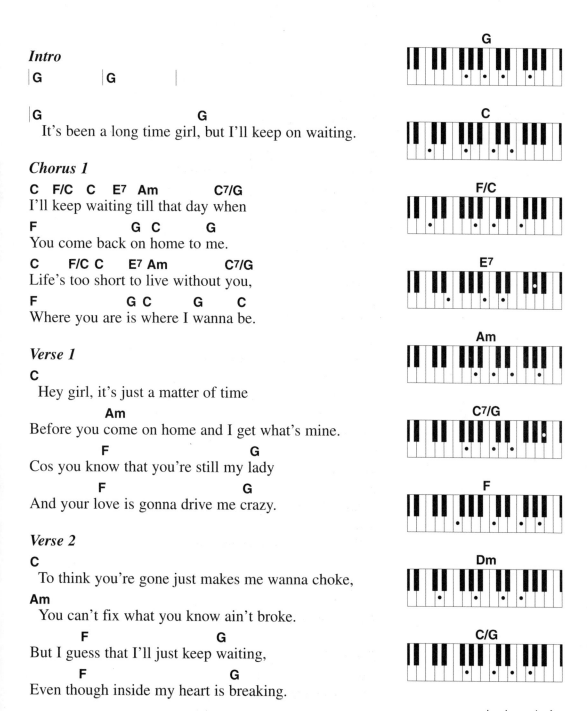

Intro

| G | G | |

|G   G
It's been a long time girl, but I'll keep on waiting.

Chorus 1

C F/C C E7 Am   C7/G
I'll keep waiting till that day when
F   G C   G
You come back on home to me.
C   F/C C   E7 Am   C7/G
Life's too short to live without you,
F   G C   G   C
Where you are is where I wanna be.

Verse 1

C
  Hey girl, it's just a matter of time
        Am
Before you come on home and I get what's mine.
      F   G
Cos you know that you're still my lady
      F   G
And your love is gonna drive me crazy.

Verse 2

C
  To think you're gone just makes me wanna choke,
Am
  You can't fix what you know ain't broke.
      F   G
But I guess that I'll just keep waiting,
      F   G
Even though inside my heart is breaking.

more chords overleaf...

Bridge 1

```
Dm                   G
What you waitin' for? (What you waitin' for girl?)
Dm                        G   C/G  G
Show me love like you did before.
```

Chorus 2

```
C  F/C  C  E7  Am          C7/G
I'll keep waiting till that day when
F              G C        G
You come back on home to me.
C     F/C  C   E7 Am          C7/G
Life's too short to live without you,
F              G C     G     C
Where you are is where I wanna be.
```

Verse 3

```
C
  All this love's too much to understand,
Am
  Must be a part of a master plan.
        F                    G
But I wish that it was just that easy,
        F                    G
Cos I miss the way you touch and tease me.
```

Verse 4

```
C
  Damn it girl, why can't you see
Am
  It's not over for you and me?
F
  One day you'll see that you were wrong,
      C                    G
Then you will realise it was true love all along.
```

Bridge 2

```
Dm                   G
Dry these tears of rain, (Dry these tears of rain)
Dm                    G    C/G  G
Say you'll show me love again.
```

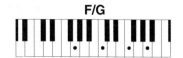
F/G

Chorus 3

C F/C C E7 Am   C7/G
I'll keep waiting till that day when

F   G C   G
You come back on home to me.

C   F/C C   E7 Am   C7/G
Life's too short to live without you,

F   G C   G
Where you are is where I wanna be.

Middle

G   F/G
  What can I say to change your mind?

G   F/G
  Thinkin' about you all of the time.

G   F/G
  Don't keep me holding on,

G   F/G   G
  Come back to where you belong.

Chorus 4

C F/C C E7 Am   C7/G
I'll keep waiting till that day when

F   C/G C   G
You come back on   home to me.

C   F/C C   E7 Am   C7/G
Life's too short to live without you,

F   G C   G   C
Where you are is where I wanna be.

Chorus 5

||:   F/C C E7 Am   C7/G
  I'll keep waiting till that day when

F   C/G C   G
You come back on   home to me.

C   F/C C   E7 Am   C7/G
Life's too short to live without you,

F   G C   G   C   :|| *Repeat to fade*
Where you are is where I wanna be.

25

I Really Miss You

Words & Music by Georgina Dennis, Eliot Kennedy & Pete Lincoln

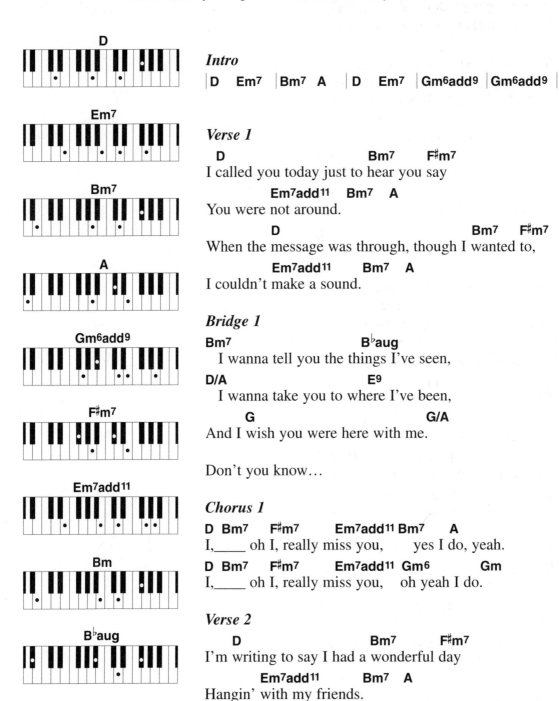

D

Em⁷

Bm⁷

A

Gm⁶add⁹

F♯m⁷

Em⁷add¹¹

Bm

B♭aug

Intro

| D Em⁷ | Bm⁷ A | D Em⁷ | Gm⁶add⁹ | Gm⁶add⁹ |

Verse 1

   D   Bm⁷   F♯m⁷
I called you today just to hear you say

        Em⁷add¹¹ Bm⁷ A
You were not around.

          D   Bm⁷ F♯m⁷
When the message was through, though I wanted to,

        Em⁷add¹¹   Bm⁷ A
I couldn't make a sound.

Bridge 1

Bm⁷   B♭aug
  I wanna tell you the things I've seen,

D/A   E⁹
  I wanna take you to where I've been,

       G   G/A
And I wish you were here with me.

Don't you know…

Chorus 1

D Bm⁷ F♯m⁷   Em⁷add¹¹ Bm⁷   A
I,____ oh I, really miss you,   yes I do, yeah.

D Bm⁷ F♯m⁷   Em⁷add¹¹ Gm⁶   Gm
I,____ oh I, really miss you, oh yeah I do.

Verse 2

   D   Bm⁷   F♯m⁷
I'm writing to say I had a wonderful day

        Em⁷add¹¹   Bm⁷ A
Hangin' with my friends.

      D   **Bm⁷**   **F♯m⁷**
But the memory dies as the sun reach the skies,

     Em⁷add¹¹ **Bm⁷**   **A**
I'm alone again.

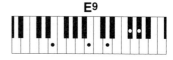

Bridge 2

Bm⁷   **B♭aug**
  I wanna tell you the weather is fine,

       D/A   **E⁹**
When the night comes around, you were on my mind,

    G   **G/A**
And I wish you were here with me.

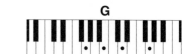

Don't you know…

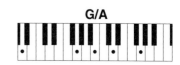

Chorus 2

D Bm⁷   **F♯m⁷**   **Em⁷add¹¹ Bm⁷**   **A**
I,____ oh I, really miss you,   yes I do, yeah.
D Bm⁷   **F♯m⁷**   **Em⁷add¹¹ Bm⁷**   **A**
I,____ oh I, really miss you,   yes I do, I miss you.
D Bm⁷   **F♯m⁷**   **Em⁷add¹¹ Gm⁶**   **Gm**
I,____ oh I, really miss you, oh yeah I do.

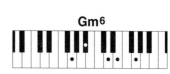

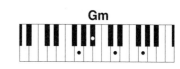

Verse 3 (Instrumental)

|**D** |**Bm⁷**   **F♯m⁷** |**Em⁷add¹¹** |**Bm⁷**   **A** |

|**D** |**Bm⁷**   **F♯m⁷** |**Em⁷add¹¹** |**Bm⁷**   **A** |

Bridge 3

Bm⁷   **B♭aug**
  I wanna tell you the things I've seen,

D/A   **E⁹**
  I wanna take you to where I've been,

    G   **G/A**
And I wish you were here with me.

Oh, don't you know that…

Chorus 3

D Bm⁷   F♯m⁷   Em⁷add¹¹ Bm⁷   A
I,____ oh I, really miss you,   yes I do, yeah.
D Bm⁷   F♯m⁷   Em⁷add¹¹ Bm⁷   A
I,____ oh I, really miss you,   I miss you.

Verse 4

     D   Bm⁷   F♯m⁷
I called you today just to hear you say
            Em⁷add¹¹   Bm⁷   A
You were not around.
                 D   Bm⁷   F♯m⁷
When the message was through, though I wanted to,
            Em⁷add¹¹   Bm⁷   A
I couldn't make a sound.

Verse 5 (to fade)

     D   Bm⁷   F♯m⁷
I'm writing to say I had a wonderful day
            Em⁷add¹¹   Bm⁷   A
Hangin' with my friends.
              D   Bm⁷   F♯m⁷
But the memory dies as the sun reach the skies,
          Em⁷add¹¹   Bm⁷   A
I'm alone again.

It's A Feel Good Thing

Words & Music by Mike Rose, Nick Foster & Kim Fuller

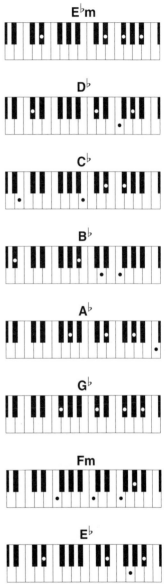

E♭m

D♭

C♭

B♭

A♭

G♭

Fm

E♭

Intro

|E♭m   D♭ |C♭   B♭ |E♭m   D♭ |C♭   B♭ |

|E♭m   D♭ |C♭   B♭ |E♭m   D♭ |C♭   B♭ |

Verse 1

E♭m   D♭   C♭   B♭
  Come join the party, come on get up off your seat,

E♭m   D♭   C♭   B♭
  Doesn't matter who you are, we all dance to the same beat,

E♭m   D♭   C♭   B♭
  Come put your hands together, shake your little feet,

       E♭m   D♭   C♭   B♭
Way-ee-yay-ee-oh! (Way-ee-yay-ee-oh!)

Bridge 1

E♭m   A♭   D♭   G♭
Buenos tiempo - with these friends of mine.

E♭m   A♭   D♭   G♭
Buenos tiempo -   we have good times.

E♭m   A♭   D♭   G♭
Buenos tiempo - it can't get no higher.

E♭m   A♭   D♭   G♭
Buenos tiempo - through the streets of fire.

Chorus 1

Fm   B♭
  And once you've started up

         E♭   A♭
You're gonna dance until you drop,

     Fm   B♭   E♭   A♭
It's a feel good thing, it's an S Club thing.

Fm   **B♭**
  And when the rhythm hits you
    E♭   **A♭**
You'll never wanna stop,
      Fm   **B♭**   **E♭**   **A♭**
It's a feel good thing, it's an S Club thing.

Link
Fm   **B♭ E♭**   **A♭**
Oh oh oh oh, oh oh oh oh,
Fm   **B♭**   **E♭**   **A♭**
Oh oh oh oh, it's a feel good thing.

Verse 2
E♭m   **D♭**   **C♭**   **B♭**
Now you're in the party mood, there's no turning back,
E♭m   **D♭**   **C♭**   **B♭**
  Just let yourself go and you'll be on the right track,
E♭m   **D♭**   **C♭**   **B♭**
Every boy and every girl holding hands around the world,
      E♭m   **D♭**   **C♭**   **B♭**
Way-ee-yay-ee-oh! (Way-ee-yay-ee-oh!)

Bridge 2
E♭m   **A♭ D♭**   **G♭**
Buenos tiempo - with these friends of mine.
E♭m   **A♭ D♭**   **G♭**
Buenos tiempo -   we have good times.
E♭m   **A♭ D♭**   **G♭**
Buenos tiempo - it can't get no higher.
E♭m   **A♭ D♭**   **G♭**
Buenos tiempo - through the streets of fire.

Chorus 2

As Chorus 1

Instrumental
| **Fm**   **B♭** | **E♭**   **A♭** | **Fm**   **B♭** | **E♭**   **A♭** |

Link 2

Fm   **B**♭ **E**♭   **A**♭
Oh oh oh oh, oh oh oh oh,

Fm   **B**♭ **E**♭   **A**♭
Oh, oh oh oh, through the streets of fire.

Chorus 3

‖: **Fm**   **B**♭
  And once you've started up

         E♭   **A**♭
You're gonna dance until you drop,

     Fm   **B**♭   **E**♭   **A**♭
It's a feel good thing, it's an S Club thing.

Fm   **B**♭
  And when the rhythm hits you

   E♭   **A**♭
You'll never wanna stop,

     Fm   **B**♭   **E**♭   **A**♭   :‖ *Repeat to fade*
It's a feel good thing, it's an S Club thing.

Reach

Words & Music by Cathy Dennis & Andrew Todd

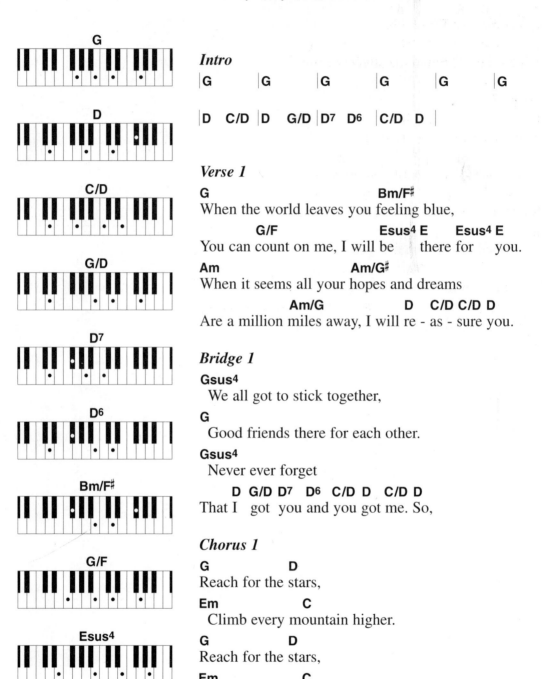

G

D

C/D

G/D

D7

D6

Bm/F♯

G/F

Esus4

Intro

|G |G |G |G |G |G |

|D C/D |D G/D |D7 D6 |C/D D |

Verse 1

G   Bm/F♯
When the world leaves you feeling blue,
            G/F   Esus4 E   Esus4 E
You can count on me, I will be   there for   you.
Am   Am/G♯
When it seems all your hopes and dreams
                    Am/G   D   C/D C/D D
Are a million miles away, I will re - as - sure you.

Bridge 1

Gsus4
   We all got to stick together,
G
   Good friends there for each other.
Gsus4
   Never ever forget
         D G/D D7   D6   C/D D   C/D D
That I   got you and you got me. So,

Chorus 1

G   D
Reach for the stars,
Em   C
   Climb every mountain higher.
G   D
Reach for the stars,
Em   C
   Follow your heart's desire.

```
G           D
Reach for the stars,
Em          F              C        | C
  And when that rainbow's shining over you,
Dsus4   D         Dsus4    D      G
  That's when your dreams will all come true.
| G      | G      | G          |
```

Verse 2

```
G                    Bm/F#
There's a place waiting just for you,
      G/F                  Esus4  E  Esus4 E
It's a special place where your dreams all come true.
Am              Am/G#
Fly away, swim the ocean blue,
      Am/G            D   C/D    D
Drive that open road, leave the past behind you.
```

Bridge 2

```
Gsus4
  Don't stop, gotta keep movin',
G
  Your hopes, gotta keep buildin'.
Gsus4
  Never ever forget
    D  G/D  D7  D6  C/D  D  C/D D
That I  got  you and you  got me. So,
```

Chorus 2

```
G           D
Reach for the stars,
Em          C
  Climb every mountain higher.
G           D
Reach for the stars,
Em          C
  Follow your heart's desire.
```

E

Am

Am/G#

Am/G

Gsus4

Em

C

F

Dsus4

F/G

Am add9

more chords overleaf...

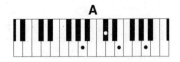

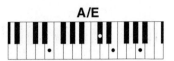

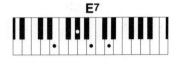

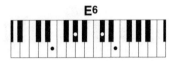

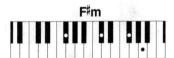

G   D
Reach for the stars,

Em   F   C |C
And when that rainbow's shining over you,

Dsus4 D   Dsus4   D   G |G
That's when your dreams will all come true.

Middle

F/G   G
Don't believe in all that you've been told,

F/G   G
The sky's the limit, you can reach your goal.

C   Am add9   Am
No one knows just what the future holds,

                     G
There ain't nothin' you can't be,

               E
There's the whole world at your feet.

Chorus 3

        A
I said reach! Climb every mountain.

A
Reach! Reach for the moon.

A
Reach! Follow that rainbow.

E A/E E7 E6   D/E   E   D/E   E
And your dreams will all come true.

Chorus 4

A   E
Reach for the stars,

F#m   D
Climb every mountain higher.

A   E
Reach for the stars,

F#m   D
Follow your heart's desire.

```
A              E
```
Reach for the stars,
```
F♯m             G              D
```
  And when that rainbow's shining over you,
```
Esus⁴ E            Esus⁴     E
```
That's when your dreams will all come true.

Chorus 5

```
‖: A              E
```
  Reach for the stars,
```
F♯m            D
```
  Climb every mountain higher.
```
A              E
```
Reach for the stars,
```
F♯m            D
```
  Follow your heart's desire.
```
A              E
```
Reach for the stars,
```
F♯m             G              D
```
  And when that rainbow's shining over you,
```
Esus⁴ E            Esus⁴     E
```
That's when your dreams will all come true. :‖ *Repeat*
                                                                  to fade

S Club Party

Words & Music by Mikkel Eriksen, Hallgeir Rustan, Tor Hermansen & Hugh Atkins

Bm⁷

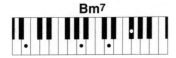

E⁷

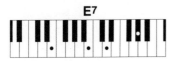

G

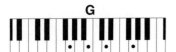

A

D

D/C♯

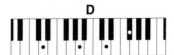

Intro

N.C.
S Club. Get down tonight, c'mon, yeah.

Get down tonight, ah ha.

Everybody get down tonight, c'mon.

Chorus 1

Bm⁷
S Club
          E⁷
(There ain't no party like an S Club party.)
        G   **A**
Gonna show you how.
D   **D/C♯**
  (Everybody get down tonight.)
Bm⁷
S Club
          E⁷
(There ain't no party like an S Club party.)
        G   **A**
Gonna take you high.
D   **D/C♯**
  (Shake your body from side to side.)

Verse 1

Bm⁷
Finally Friday night,
          E⁷
Feelin' kinda good, lookin' alright.
        Bm⁷
Gotta get movin', can't be late,
        E⁷
Gotta get groovin', just can't wait.

more chords overleaf…

Bm⁷
(Get the feeling) Get the feeling,

E⁷
(Push the ceiling) Push the ceiling,

Bm⁷
(Player haters) Player haters,

    E⁷ N.C.
Get ready everybody cos here we go.

Chorus 2

As Chorus 1

Middle 1
Bm⁷
Ooh, ooh, throw your hands in the air.

E⁷
Ooh, ooh, like you just don't care.

Bm⁷
Ooh, ooh, it's a party over here,

E⁷
Ooh, ooh, it's a party over there.

Verse 2
Bm⁷
Tina's doing her dance,

E⁷
Jon's looking for romance,

Bm⁷
Paul's getting down on the floor

    E⁷
While Hannah's screaming out for more.

Bm⁷
Wanna see Bradley swing?

    E⁷
Wanna see Rachel do her thing?

      Bm⁷
Then we got Jo, she's got the flow,

  E⁷ N.C.
Get ready everybody cos here we go.

Chorus 3

Bm7
S Club

      E7
(There ain't no party like an S Club party.)

      G   **A**
Gonna show you how.

D   **D/C♯**
  (Everybody get down tonight.)

Bm7
S Club

      E7
(There ain't no party like an S Club party.)

      G   **A**
Gonna take you high.

D   **D/C♯**
  (Shake your body from side to side.)

Middle 2

Bm7
Ooh, ooh, wave your hands in the air.

E7
Ooh, ooh, like you just don't care.

Bm7
Ooh, ooh, it's a party over here,

E7
Ooh, ooh, it's a party over there.

Middle 3

As Middle 2

Bridge

Bm7   **E7**
Ghetto boys, make some noise.

Bm7   **E7** **N.C.**
Hoochie mamas, show your nanas.

Chorus 4

Bm7
S Club

  E7
(There ain't no party like an S Club party.)

   G   **A**
Gonna show you how.

D
 (Everybody get down tonight.)

Chorus 5

‖: **C#m7**
 S Club

  F#7
(There ain't no party like an S Club party.)

   A   **B**
Gonna show you how.

E   **E/D#**
 (Everybody get down tonight.)

  C#m7
S Club

  F#7
(There ain't no party like an S Club party.)

   A   **B**
Gonna take you high.

E   **E/D#** :‖ *Repeat to fade*
 (Shake your body from side to side.)

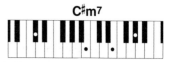

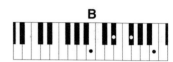

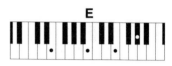

Natural

Words & Music by Norma Ray, Jean Fredenucci, Cathy Dennis & Andrew Todd
'Natural' is adapted from the song 'Tous Les Maux D'Amour' (Words & Music by Norma Ray & Jean Fredenucci). Contains an extract of 'Pavane' by Gabriel Fauré.

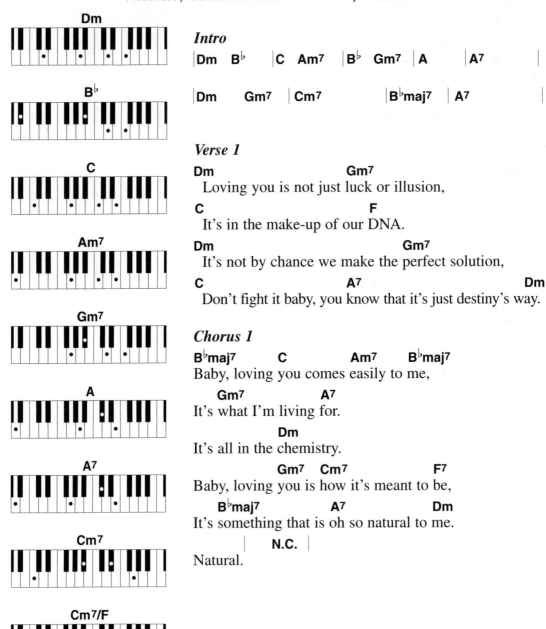

Dm

B♭

C

Am⁷

Gm⁷

A

A⁷

Cm⁷

Cm⁷/F

Intro

|Dm   B♭ |C   Am⁷ |B♭   Gm⁷ |A |A⁷ |

|Dm   Gm⁷ |Cm⁷ |B♭maj⁷ |A⁷ |

Verse 1

Dm   Gm⁷
  Loving you is not just luck or illusion,
C   F
  It's in the make-up of our DNA.
Dm   Gm⁷
  It's not by chance we make the perfect solution,
C   A⁷   Dm
  Don't fight it baby, you know that it's just destiny's way.

Chorus 1

B♭maj⁷   C   Am⁷   B♭maj⁷
Baby, loving you comes easily to me,
     Gm⁷   A⁷
It's what I'm living for.
                Dm
It's all in the chemistry.
              Gm⁷ Cm⁷   F⁷
Baby, loving you is how it's meant to be,
     B♭maj⁷   A⁷   Dm
It's something that is oh so natural to me.
           | N.C. |
Natural.

© Copyright 2000 M6 Interactions/BRJ Music/Jean Fredenucci/EMI Music Publishing Limited,
127 Charing Cross Road, London WC2 (92.5%)/
BMG Music Publishing Limited, Bedford House, 69-79 Fulham High Street, London SW6 (7.5%).
This arrangement © Copyright 2000 BMG Music Publishing Limited for their share of interest.
All Rights Reserved. International Copyright Secured.

Verse 2

Dm   **Gm7**
  We got the answers but there's no explanation,
C   **F**
  We got each other baby, come what may.
Dm   **Gm7**
  It's in the science, it's genetically proven,
C   **A7**   **Dm**
  Cos when you touch me, the reaction, it just blows me away.

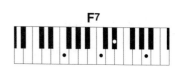

Chorus 2

B♭maj7   **C**   **Am7**   **B♭maj7**
Baby, loving you comes easily to me,
    Gm7   **A7**
It's what I'm living for.
              Dm
It's all in the chemistry.
              Gm7   **Cm7**   **F7**
Baby, loving you is how it's meant to be,
    B♭maj7   **A7**   **Dm**
It's something that is oh so natural to me.

Chorus 3

B♭maj7   **C**   **Am7**   **B♭maj7**
Baby, loving you comes easily to me,
    Gm7   **A7**
It's what I'm living for.
              Dm
It's all in the chemistry.
              Gm7   **Cm7**   **F7**
Baby, loving you is how it's meant to be,
    B♭maj7   **A7**   **Dm**
It's something that is oh so natural to me.
          | **N.C.** |
Natural.

Middle

Dm   Gm7
  Turn off the light, lay your head next to mine.

C   F
  Take it slowly, a step at a time.

Dm   Gm7
  C'mon, get close, closer to me,

C   A7   Dm
  It's oh so natural,   it's oh so easy to see.

Chorus 4

‖: B♭maj7   C   Am7   B♭maj7
  Baby, loving you comes easily to me,

   Gm7   A7
It's what I'm living for.

                  Dm
It's all in the chemistry.

               Gm7 Cm7   F7
Baby, loving you is how it's meant to be,

   B♭maj7   A7   Dm :‖ *Repeat to fade*
It's something that is oh so natural to me.

You're My Number One

Words & Music by Mike Rose & Nick Foster

E♭

Fm7/E♭

E♭maj7

A♭/E♭

A♭

B♭/A♭

Gm7

Cm

Fm7

Intro

| N.C. | N.C.

E♭   Fm7/E♭
Ooh._____

E♭maj7 Fm7/E♭
Ooh._____

E♭   Fm7/E♭   E♭
Na na na na na na na na na
          A♭/E♭
Na na na na na na na.

Verse 1

E♭   Fm7/E♭
What is love? Cos baby, I don't know,
      E♭   A♭/E♭
I got a funny feeling in my heart.
      E♭   Fm7/E♭
If this is love, it feels like butterflies,
            E♭   A♭/E♭
So tell me baby, is this how it starts?

Bridge 1

A♭   B♭/A♭
   I know I've never felt like this before,
Gm7   Cm
   You're like a drug, you got me wanting more,
      Fm7
I've got to let you know,
         B♭11   B♭
I've got to let you know.

more chords overleaf...

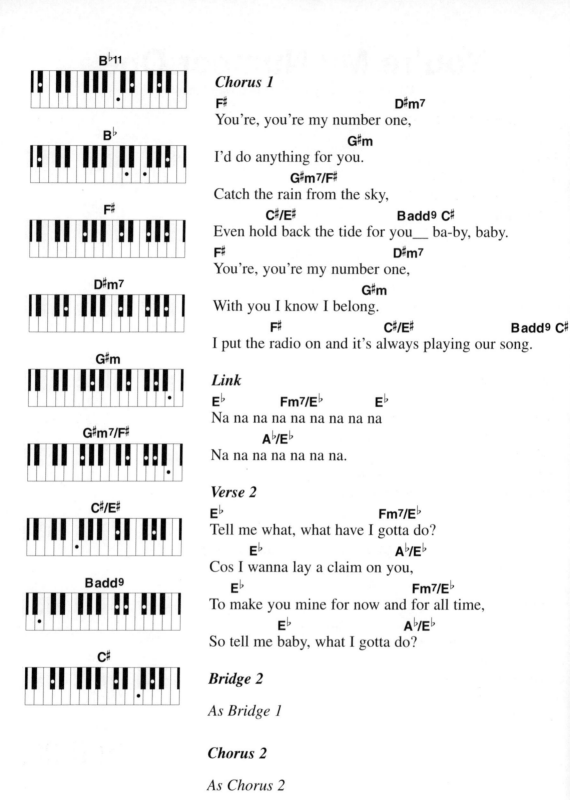

Chorus 1

F#   D#m7
You're, you're my number one,

                             G#m
I'd do anything for you.

                            G#m7/F#
Catch the rain from the sky,

                    C#/E#   Badd9 C#
Even hold back the tide for you__ ba-by, baby.

F#   D#m7
You're, you're my number one,

                             G#m
With you I know I belong.

        F#   C#/E#   Badd9 C#
I put the radio on and it's always playing our song.

Link

E♭   Fm7/E♭   E♭
Na na na na na na na na na

          A♭/E♭
Na na na na na na na.

Verse 2

E♭   Fm7/E♭
Tell me what, what have I gotta do?

      E♭   A♭/E♭
Cos I wanna lay a claim on you,

      E♭   Fm7/E♭
To make you mine for now and for all time,

        E♭   A♭/E♭
So tell me baby, what I gotta do?

Bridge 2

As Bridge 1

Chorus 2

As Chorus 2

Middle

B   F#/A#   C#
  There ain't nothing I won't do.

 G#m A#m
(Ooh_____)

B   F#/A#   G#
  I'd walk on water just to be with you.

F#/C# C#
(Ooh_____)

N.C. B C#
     Baby, baby.

Chorus 3

‖: F#   D#m7
  You're, you're my number one,

       G#m
I'd do anything for you.

      G#m7/F#
Catch the rain from the sky,

    C#/E#   Badd9 C#
Even hold back the tide for you baby, baby.

F#   D#m7
You're, you're my number one,

      G#m
With you I know I belong.   *Repeat to fade*

   F#   C#/E#   Badd9 C# :‖
I put the radio on and it's always playing our song.

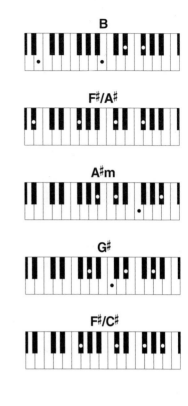

B

F#/A#

A#m

G#

F#/C#

45

Two In A Million

Words & Music by Cathy Dennis & Simon Ellis

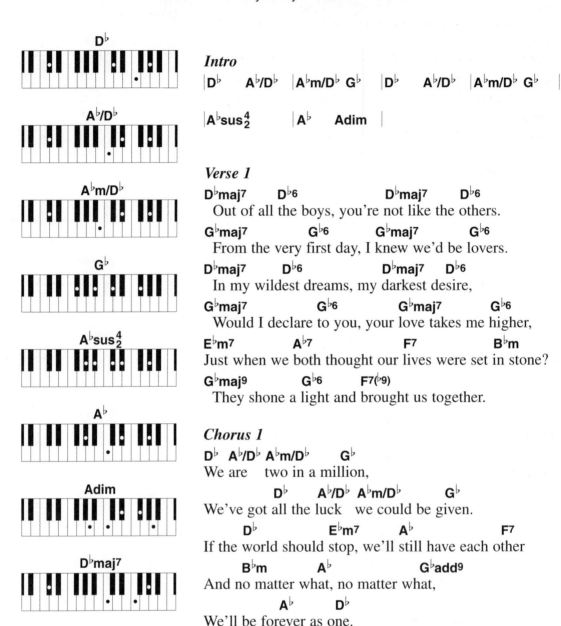

Intro

|D♭ A♭/D♭ |A♭m/D♭ G♭ |D♭ A♭/D♭ |A♭m/D♭ G♭ |

|A♭sus$^4_2$ |A♭ Adim |

Verse 1

D♭maj7   D♭6   D♭maj7   D♭6
Out of all the boys, you're not like the others.
G♭maj7   G♭6   G♭maj7   G♭6
From the very first day, I knew we'd be lovers.
D♭maj7   D♭6   D♭maj7   D♭6
In my wildest dreams, my darkest desire,
G♭maj7   G♭6   G♭maj7   G♭6
Would I declare to you, your love takes me higher,
E♭m7   A♭7   F7   B♭m
Just when we both thought our lives were set in stone?
G♭maj9   G♭6   F7(♭9)
They shone a light and brought us together.

Chorus 1

D♭ A♭/D♭ A♭m/D♭   G♭
We are   two in a million,
            D♭   A♭/D♭ A♭m/D♭   G♭
We've got all the luck   we could be given.
         D♭   E♭m7   A♭   F7
If the world should stop, we'll still have each other
         B♭m   A♭   G♭add9
And no matter what, no matter what,
         A♭   D♭
We'll be forever as one.

Verse 2

D♭maj7   D♭6   D♭maj7   D♭6
  It's a crazy world where everything's changing.

G♭maj7   G♭6   G♭maj7   G♭6
  One minute you're up and the next thing you're breaking.

D♭maj7   D♭6   D♭maj7   D♭6
  When I lose my way and the skies they get heavy,

G♭maj7   G♭6   G♭maj7   G♭6
  It'd be O.K. the moment you're with me.

E♭m7   A♭7   F7   B♭m
  No one would have guessed we'd be standing strong today,

G♭maj9   G♭6   F7(♭9)
  Solid as a rock and perfect in every way.

Chorus 2

D♭ A♭/D♭ A♭m/D♭   G♭
We are   two in a million,

          D♭   A♭/D♭ A♭m/D♭   G♭
We've got all the luck we could be given.

       D♭   E♭m7   A♭   F7
If the world should stop, we'll still have each other

    B♭m   A♭   G♭add9
And no matter what, no matter what,

       A♭   A♭sus$^4_2$
We'll be forever as one,

A♭   A♭sus$^4_2$ | A♭   Adim
  Forever as one.

Chorus 3

‖: D♭ A♭/D♭ A♭m/D♭   G♭
  We are   two in a million,

          D♭   A♭/D♭ A♭m/D♭   G♭
We've got all the luck we could be given.

       D♭   E♭m7   A♭   F7
If the world should stop, we'll still have each other

    B♭m   A♭ G♭add9
And no matter what,

       A♭   D♭   :‖
We'll be forever as one.

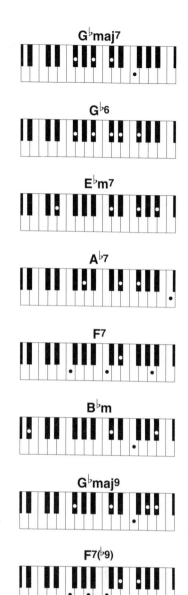

G♭maj7

G♭6

E♭m7

A♭7

F7

B♭m

G♭maj9

F7(♭9)

G♭add9

Chorus 4

D♭ A♭/D♭ A♭m/D♭   G♭
We are   two in a million,

                D♭   A♭/D♭ A♭m/D♭   G♭
We've got all the luck we could be given.

        D♭   E♭m7   A♭   F7
If the world should stop, we'll still have each other

    B♭m   A♭   G♭add9
And no matter what, no matter what,

           A♭
We'll be forever as...

  B♭m   A♭   G♭add9
No matter what, no matter what,

           A♭
We'll be forever as...

  B♭m   A♭   G♭add9
No matter what, no matter what,

           A♭   D♭
We'll be forever as one.

A2 Sociology
UNIT 2536

OCR

Module 2536
Power and Control: Crime and Deviance

Steve Chapman

To all my past and present students, and to Olive Jones for her faith in me over the years

Philip Allan Updates
Market Place
Deddington
Oxfordshire
OX15 0SE

tel: 01869 338652
fax: 01869 337590
e-mail: sales@philipallan.co.uk
www.philipallan.co.uk

ISBN 0 86003 921 8

This Guide has been written specifically to support students preparing for the OCR A2 Sociology Unit 2536 examination. The content has been neither approved nor endorsed by OCR and remains the sole responsibility of the author.

Typeset by Good Imprint, East Grinstead, West Sussex
Printed by Information Press, Eynsham, Oxford

Contents

Introduction

About this guide 4

The A2 specification 5

Examinable skills 5

Study skills and revision strategies 7

The unit test 8

■ ■ ■

Content Guidance

About this section 12

Patterns of crime and victimisation
Patterns of crime by social profile 13

Measuring crime and issues of reliability and validity 14

Power, control and criminalisation 19

Patterns of victimisation 24

Sociological explanations of crime and deviance
Structuralist theories 28

Interactionist approaches 39

Realist approaches 44

Feminist approaches 48

Explanations for ethnic-minority crime 52

■ ■ ■

Questions and Answers

About this section 58

Q1 The role of the mass media in defining crime and deviance 59

Q2 Structuralist theories of crime 66

Q3 Measuring crime 74

Q4 Realist explanations of crime 81

Q5 Gender and crime 86

Q6 Ethnicity and crime 87

Introduction

About this guide

This unit guide is for students following the OCR A2 Sociology course. It deals with the **Crime and Deviance** topic which is one option included in the **Power and Control** Module 2536. This topic is designed to give you an understanding of the sociological theories, concepts and evidence relating to the underlying processes which shape crime and deviance in contemporary Britain. The emphasis is on how governments and sociologists collect information about the extent and social character of crime and criminals in the UK and particularly how crime may be influenced by factors such as social class, gender and ethnicity. This option is therefore concerned with exploring sociological theories of why particular individuals and social groups may be more prone to committing crime or engaging in what society defines as deviant activities. In this sense, you should be aware that material from this unit, especially that relating to social class, gender and ethnic inequalities, is useful evidence to collect for use in the synoptic examination. Finally, this unit also looks at how society controls the behaviour of its members through the use of such agencies as the police, prisons and judiciary.

There are three sections in this guide:

- **Introduction** — this provides advice on how to use this unit guide, an explanation of the skills required in A2 Sociology and suggestions for effective revision. It concludes with guidance on how to succeed in the unit test.
- **Content Guidance** — this provides an outline of what is included in the specification for Crime and Deviance. It is designed to make you aware of what you should know before the unit test.
- **Questions and Answers** — this provides some exam-type questions on Crime and Deviance for you to try, together with some sample answers at grade-A and grade-C level. Examiner's comments are included on how the marks are awarded.

How to use the guide

To use this guide to your best advantage, you should refer to the Introduction and Content Guidance sections from the beginning of your study of Crime and Deviance. However, in order to get full advantage from the Question and Answer section, you would be advised to wait until you have completed your study of the topic, as the questions are wide-ranging. When you are ready to use this section, you should take each question in turn, study it carefully, and write a full answer. When you have done this, study the grade-A candidate's answer and compare it with your own, paying close attention to the examiner's comments. You could also look at the grade-C answers and, using the examiner's comments as a guide, work out how to rewrite them to gain higher marks.

These tasks are quite intensive and time-consuming, so do not try to tackle all the questions at once or in a short space of time. It would be better to focus on one at a time, and spread the workload over several weeks — you can always find some time to do this, even while studying another topic. In addition to using the questions to consolidate your own knowledge and develop your exam skills, you should use at least some of the questions as revision practice — even just reading through the grade-A candidates' answers should provide you with useful revision material.

The A2 specification

The aims of the OCR A2 Sociology specification are:
- to develop in you an applied sociological knowledge and understanding of the concepts underpinning contemporary social processes and structures that are relevant to your social identity and your experiences of the social world in the twenty-first century
- to equip you with an in-depth theoretical awareness of how sociological perspectives explain the world you live in, and how these interact to provide us with an integrated set of ideas about how society operates
- to examine how sociologists collect information about the social world in which you live and whether their views on how your everyday world is organised are truthful and worthwhile
- to equip you with the necessary skills to engage in sociological debate, especially in terms of being able to interpret, apply and evaluate relevant evidence and to construct convincing sociological arguments
- to develop in you an appreciation and understanding that sociology is an interconnected academic discipline that requires you to make links between different topic areas, especially with regard to inequality and difference, and methods of sociological enquiry

Examinable skills

There are three main examinable skills in the A2 specifications, divided into two **Assessment Objectives**.

Assessment Objective 1

Assessment Objective 1 (AO1) is **knowledge and understanding**, which accounts for 46% of A2 marks on offer. Grade-A candidates are expected to demonstrate a wide-ranging and detailed knowledge of relevant sociological theories, concepts, methods and different types of evidence, especially statistical data and empirical studies. You will also need to demonstrate a holistic understanding of how the topic of Crime and Deviance is related to the synoptic unit Social Inequality and Difference.

It is important that your acquisition of knowledge goes beyond learning by rote. You also need to demonstrate a clear understanding of what you are describing. In other words, you will be expected to discuss or debate the merits of particular arguments in an organised fashion. Generally this is displayed by learning and using knowledge which is appropriate and relevant to the question set. A good way of doing this is to ask yourself the following questions:

- Do I know the main arguments in the area I am studying?
- Do I know the main sociologists who have contributed to debate in this area?
- Do I know the historical context in which these sociologists are writing?
- Do I understand the concepts used by these sociologists?
- Do I know the empirical studies and data that can be used as evidence to support or undermine particular sociological arguments?

Assessment Objective 2

Assessment Objective 2 (AO2) is broken down into **AO2 (a) interpretation and analysis**, which is worth 27% of A2 marks on offer, and **AO2 (b) evaluation**, which is also worth 27% of the total A2 marks.

Interpretation and analysis essentially involves showing the ability to select and analyse different types of evidence and data. In particular, it involves the ability to address the specifics of the question that has been set by applying and linking socio-logical evidence to specific sociological arguments or theory. It is useful to ask yourself the following questions when working out whether you have acquired this skill:

- What knowledge in the form of studies, concepts etc., is relevant when addressing a particular debate?
- Can I distinguish between facts and opinions?
- Am I capable of identifying patterns and trends in sociological data and uncovering hidden meanings?
- Am I addressing the question throughout the response?
- Have I applied contemporary issues and debates to the question?
- What evidence in the form of sociological studies and statistical data can I use to support or criticise particular arguments?
- Have I put too much of my personal opinion into my response?

Evaluation normally involves assessing the validity of particular sociological arguments and available evidence and data in a balanced way. The ability to examine critically the reliability of the methods used to collect evidence is also very important. The skill of evaluation is an essential one, and should be applied to all the material you come across during your study of the topic. It is useful to ask yourself the following questions when practising this skill:

- How many sides to the debate can be identified in this topic area?
- How was the evidence gathered?
- Can the evidence be checked?
- Is there any other evidence relating to this?
- Is the research relevant to contemporary society?

- Who does not agree with this view and why?
- Which evidence and arguments are most convincing and why?
- What have particular sociologists got to gain from saying what they do?
- Are class, gender and ethnicity taken into account?
- What are the strengths of the main argument?

In more practical terms, evaluation means that whenever you are introduced to a sociological perspective or study, you should find and learn at least three criticisms that have been made of it and two strengths. It is important to understand that evaluation can be made up of specific criticisms of a particular theory and its supporting evidence or its methods of data collection, and/or alternative theories which can used as a point of contrast. However, evaluation can be positive too. Finally, you will need to be flexible. Do not just apply all the strengths and weaknesses you have learned to the debate. Be willing to adapt them so that they make sense according to the sociological context.

Study skills and revision strategies

Good preparation for revision actually starts the minute you begin to study sociology. One of the most important revision aids that you will have is your sociology folder, so it is important that you keep this in good order. Essentially, it should be divided into topic areas. It should contain all your class notes, handouts, notes you have made from textbooks, class and homework exercises and, of course, all your marked and returned work. If you are not tidy by nature, you may find that you have to rewrite notes you make in class into a legible and coherent form before putting them in your folder. Be warned, though — this is something you should do straight away, as even after only a few days you will have forgotten things. If you keep a good folder throughout, reading through this will form a major part of your revision. In addition, you will, of course, need to reread the relevant parts of your textbooks. Your own work also forms an important revision resource. Go back over your essays and exam answers, read your teacher's comments, and use these to see whether you can redo any pieces that did not score particularly high marks.

You should always write down the definition of a concept when you first come across it — use a separate part of your folder for this. In addition, it is useful to make a brief summary of research studies, particularly those not found in your textbook. Remember to include the title, author(s) and, most importantly, the date, along with your summary of the method(s) used and the main findings. These should be kept in a section in your sociology folder, or you may wish to record them on a set of index cards.

Another important aspect of revision is to practise writing answers within the appropriate time limit. Make sure you have sufficient time not only to complete all the parts of the question, but also to reread your answer, in order to correct any careless mistakes that may have crept in while working under pressure.

Finally, you need to ensure that you have a thorough understanding of a range of appropriate theories, concepts and studies. Comprehensive revision is not something that can be done the night before the exam — you should start at least 3 weeks before. Construct a revision timetable in order to plan your topics. One way would be to aim to revise 90 minutes an evening Monday to Thursday, take Friday night off, and do 3 hours of revision over the weekend. It is advisable to revise in concentrated bursts of time. People differ in this respect, but it is seldom a good idea to spend more than 1 hour at a time on revision. Adopt a carrot and stick policy. Revise for an hour and then reward yourself with a television programme, a snack, some exercise or by listening to some music. Vary your revision programme too. You could, for example, spend 45 minutes revising theories of crime and another three quarters of an hour revising some aspect of crime and deviance, e.g. victimology, which has the advantage of also acting as evidence for the synoptic unit Social Inequality and Difference. The weekend revision session should involve setting aside some time to have a go at a question under timed conditions. It is important that you practise recall under timed conditions as much as possible.

The unit test

Crime and Deviance is one of six options available as part of Module 2536 Power and Control. The unit examination will contain a choice of 12 essay questions, two drawn from each of the six options. There will therefore be two essays drawn from Crime and Deviance. You will have to answer one of these essays in 1 hour. The unit as a whole is worth 15% of the full A-level. The essay is worth 60 marks in all, composed of 28 marks for AO1 (knowledge and understanding), 16 marks for AO2 (a) (interpretation and analysis) and 16 marks for AO2 (b) (evaluation).

Each essay will use the command words **outline and assess** and refer to a particular sociological view, explanation or theory relating to some aspect of the crime and deviance specifications. It is important that you think carefully about the organisation and structure of your essay.

- It is a good idea to begin by constructing an introduction that 'sets the scene'. This should aim to explain the point of view contained in the question, to define any technical terms used in the question and to identify the key players in terms of sociologists/theories involved in the debate.
- You should then spend time explaining the view embodied in the question by outlining the key features of particular sociological positions. It is sometimes useful to do this by first outlining the theoretical argument(s) and then supporting these with empirical sociological studies or statistical data. Throughout this stage it is important that you clearly link whatever it is you are discussing to the view contained in the question.
- Once you have outlined and supported the view contained in the question, you can address the evaluation of that view. Note that there are 16 marks available

for this skill, so your critical appraisal must be fairly substantial. You may like to begin by addressing specific features of the theories/studies/data already discussed which you think are problematic. The key here is to make sure that the examiner knows that you are engaged in evaluation, so use evaluative words or phrases to draw attention to this, e.g. 'however'. Remember that evaluation can also be positive. If the theory has strengths, discuss these too.

- The next step is to outline any alternative theories with supporting evidence that challenge the view in the question. Make sure, however, that you state clearly how the alternative set of theories is challenging the previous position. A common error is to forget to do this.

- Finally, try and finish with some sort of conclusion. There are two types. You may elect to go for a summative conclusion and merely remind the examiner of the competing positions and how they generally differ. You may prefer an evaluative conclusion in which you make a judgement based on the evidence as to which position has more validity as a convincing argument.

You have 60 minutes to spend on this question. You should aim to spend about 5 minutes planning your response and approximately 50 minutes writing. You should aim to fill at least four sides of the answer book.

Content
Guidance

This section is intended to show you the major issues and themes covered in **Crime and Deviance**. However, it is not an exhaustive or comprehensive list of the key concepts, issues and sociological studies that you could use to answer questions on this topic. Rather it is an outline of the key concepts that you need to know plus guidance on some issues and sociological studies that are worth further investigation. You should be able to access further information by consulting your teacher, and by referring to your textbook and past copies of *Sociology Review*.

The content of the **Crime and Deviance** option falls into six main areas which cut across the three main sections outlined in the specifications:

- **defining and measuring official criminal statistics**
- **assessing the role of mass media and agents of social control such as the police and the courts in the criminalisation of particular social groups**
- **explaining social class differences in crime rates**
- **explaining age differences in crime rates**
- **explaining gender differences in crime rates**
- **explaining ethnic differences in crime rates**

The topic is designed to give you a good understanding of the underlying processes which shape the potential of particular individuals and social groups to engage in criminal and deviant activities. It examines how society defines and measures both crime and deviance and pays close attention to how information about crime is collected and, in particular, to methodological key concepts such as reliability and validity which underpin collection of data about crime. This unit also examines the sociological theories which purport to explain why some social groups such as males, the working class, young people and African-Caribbeans are more likely to engage in crime while commenting on why other social groups such as females, Asians and members of the middle class are less likely to show up in the official criminal statistics. Finally, the unit examines the social control functions of agencies such as the police, prisons and judiciary.

You should be aware of three key aspects of the Crime and Deviance option when you start revising this unit and using the information below. First, you should become familiar with, and be able to apply accurately, key concepts and theories that underpin the central topic areas in this unit, and to support them, whenever possible, with empirical sociological studies. You particularly need to have a detailed knowledge and understanding of theory. Second, you should develop an evaluative understanding of key concepts, theories and studies. Evaluation as a skill is highly rewarded at this level. Third, it is important to have a 'synoptic awareness', i.e. to know how evidence from this topic area might be used to support the view that class, gender and ethnic inequalities exist. This will help you to answer question (d) of the synoptic examination.

Patterns of crime and victimisation

The official criminal statistics are collected by the police and the courts and collated and published by the Home Office. They are used to establish trends and patterns in criminal activity, especially with regard to the volume of crime and the social characteristics of criminality. Some of the trends are as follows:

- Between 1971 and 1993 there was a dramatic rise in the volume of recorded crime in the UK, and all major categories of crime experienced substantial increases, e.g. violent crime increased four-fold in this period.
- Between 1993 and 1999 the crime rate fell significantly, despite the fact that the general public, fuelled by the media, believed it was rising.
- Since 1999 property crime has generally fallen, although violent crime against the person has risen so that it now constitutes 15% of all crime.
- Property crime, however, still makes up the major proportion of crime.

Patterns of crime by social profile

If we examine the official criminal statistics in terms of those being arrested, charged and convicted, we can see that some social groups are more likely to appear than others.

Age

- The peak age for known offenders for both males and females was 14 in 1958 and 18 in 1997.
- The official statistics show that juvenile crime has declined in recent years after reaching a peak in 1984/85. In 1958, 56% of all offenders found guilty were aged 20 years or under compared with 38% in 1997.
- However, the official criminal statistics indicate that burglary, street robbery, shoplifting and criminal damage are likely to be juvenile rather than adult offences.

Social class

- Examination of the employment status of convicted offenders suggests that over 80% are from the manual classes.
- Coleman and Moynihan (1996) found that offenders tend to live in the most economically deprived areas.
- Hagell and Newburn's study of persistent young offenders (1996) found that only 8% came from middle-class backgrounds.
- Offences are also distinguishable by social class. Middle-class offenders tend to be associated with white-collar crime, fraud and tax evasion, while working-class offenders are mainly found guilty of burglary and street crime.

Ethnicity

- The statistics show an over-representation of ethnic-minority men and women, and particularly African-Caribbeans, in prison.
- Approximately one-tenth of male prisoners and one-fifth of female prisoners in UK prisons are African-Caribbean yet this ethnic-minority group makes up only 2.3% of the population.
- Smith (1997) notes that black youth are more likely to be cautioned than any other ethnic minority group.

Gender

- The number of female offenders has risen faster than the number of male offenders since 1958, but approximately 80%–90% of offenders found guilty or cautioned are male.
- At least one-third of men are likely to be convicted for a criminal offence before the age of 35, compared with only 8% of women.
- The ratio of male crime to female crime is approximately 5 to 1.
- Men are convicted for all types of offence whereas when females are convicted it is likely to be for theft (shoplifting).
- Women dominate the numbers for only two offences: prostitution and failing to obtain a television licence.
- Women are generally convicted of less serious offences than men.

Region

- Urban areas, especially inner-city council estates, have higher rates of crime than the suburbs or rural areas. The poor therefore stand a greater chance than any other social group of being victims of crime.
- Official surveys on crime risks indicate that members of young households living in inner cities, e.g. students, are ten times more likely to be burgled than older people living in rural areas.

Measuring crime and issues of reliability and validity

The interpretivist critique

Interpretivist sociologists have long questioned the reliability and validity of the official criminal statistics (as have senior police officers).

- The methods by which such data are collected, i.e. victims reporting crime and police officers detecting crime, are thought to be unreliable. For example, the 43 police forces of the UK do not collect information about crime in a standardised universal fashion.

content guidance

- Moreover, the picture of crime and criminals that is generated by such methods is thought to be lacking in validity. The 'typical' criminal outlined above and based upon the official criminal statistics may not be a realistic reflection of who is committing crime in the UK.
- Interpretivist sociologists argue that the official criminal statistics do not measure actual crime — rather they are a social construction, i.e. the end product of a complex and highly selective process involving interaction between several groups including the general public, victims of crime, politicians and civil servants, the mass media, chief constables and police officers, magistrates and judges, and those who make the laws and define what counts as crime, i.e. the ruling class. Interpretivists therefore argue that the official criminal statistics tell us more about the groups involved in their collection than they do about crime and criminality.

Key concepts

reliability; validity; social construction; interpretivism

The dark figure of crime

The official criminal statistics do not account for all the crime committed in the UK, only for that which is recognised as such by the victims and detected by the police. Sociologists have long argued that there exists a 'dark figure' (sometimes referred to as 'the hidden iceberg') of unrecorded crime. It may be that the social characteristics of those who are not reported or caught may differ from those who are.

- Pilkington (1996) notes that the official criminal statistics are not a complete record of crime in the UK because they only cover 'notifiable' offences or those defined as serious by the Home Office. Almost all the more minor summary offences dealt with by magistrate's courts are excluded, as are criminal offences dealt with by the Inland Revenue and Customs and Excise such as tax, VAT or excise fraud.
- The amount of actual and hidden crime is difficult to gauge because of the official counting rules set out by civil servants in the Home Office which govern how police forces record certain types of crimes. These counting rules change fairly frequently. For example, in April 1998 changes to the counting rules resulted in a dramatic apparent increase in certain types of crime, particularly violent crime, as certain types of assault traditionally defined as summary offences were upgraded to become notifiable offences. Such changes make it extremely difficult to compare crime statistics from one year to the next.
- Changes in the law also make it difficult to interpret statistics. For example, marital rape was made illegal in 1992. Any increase in rape after that year may merely reflect the extension of the law and the consequent reporting of rape by wives.
- The police may exercise discretion in terms of how they define and consequently count crime because of political pressures, both local and national, to improve their clear-up rates (e.g. police clear-up rates for burglary hover around the 10% mark across the country) or efficiency. Crimes may be redefined by the police as less serious, e.g. attempted burglary and car theft may be defined as criminal damage. Some crimes may not be recorded because the police regard them as being too trivial to classify.

- Some offenders belong to institutions, such as the armed services and prisons, which police and punish criminals outside the legal system. Public and state schools, professional associations such as the British Medical Association and the Law Society, and financial institutions such as banks, prefer not to involve the police and courts because of the bad publicity generated for their institutions. For example, schools may expel or suspend pupils for criminal activity, such as vandalism and drugs, and not involve the police. These crimes will therefore not show up in the official statistics.
- It is estimated by criminologists that for every 100 crimes committed, only 47 are reported to the police, 27 recorded by the police, and only five cleared up in the form of a caution or conviction.

Self-report studies

Some sociologists have used self-reports in an attempt to uncover the true amount of crime in society. These usually involve asking people to give information about their past illegal activities in response to a questionnaire which stresses confidentiality and anonymity. These studies, e.g. Belson (1976) on adolescent boys in London, Campbell (1984) on girls, indicate that the majority of people admit to some kind of illegal activity, which suggests that the official crime statistics should be higher. Moreover, these studies challenge the picture of the typical criminal as being male and working class. Self-reports indicate that females and middle-class males are just as likely to commit crime.

> **Evaluation**
>
> + The confidentiality and anonymity guaranteed to respondents may result in more valid data being gathered.
> - Marsh (1990) notes that self-report studies suffer from problems of reliability because people may not admit committing criminal offences even if they are guaranteed confidentiality.
> - The scope of self-reports is limited in that they are largely applied to young people. It would be difficult to get businessmen, for example, to admit to white-collar crime by this method.
> - People are unlikely to cooperate fully with questionnaires concerning sensitive and loaded issues such as domestic violence.
> - In some cases respondents, especially males, may exaggerate their delinquencies out of bravado.
> - Others may under-report due to dishonesty, forgetfulness or paranoia.
> - Attempts to check the 'honesty' of respondents have indicated that about a quarter of them are liable to conceal wrong-doings.
> - It is impossible to include all criminal acts in a questionnaire or interview, so the researcher has to be selective. This raises problems as to which offences should be included and which should not.
> - The samples for many self-report studies are unrepresentative. They are often carried out in schools but tend to exclude school drop-outs and truants.

Consequently, more delinquent groups are least likely to complete the question-naires.

Key concepts

dark figure of crime; discretion; self-reports

The effects of social and economic change on the reporting of crime

Over 80% of all recorded crimes result from reports by the public, but such reporting is not consistent and is therefore unreliable. Increases in the crime rate may quite simply reflect greater willingness by the general public and victims to report crime. There is some evidence that reporting is influenced by social and economic change.

- Social change means that the general public has become intolerant of certain types of crime, e.g. domestic and racial violence, and is therefore more likely to report it.
- Economic change, especially increased affluence, has led to greater amounts of consumer goods in people's homes and possibly greater intolerance of theft and a greater willingness to report it.
- Increased take-up of insurance encourages greater reporting by victims of property crime and criminal damage.

Victims of crime

Some criminologists suggest that the official criminal statistics may tell us more about the victims of crime than they tell us about crime and criminals. For example, the view that there is a dark figure of crime is supported by research, which suggests victims may not report crimes for various reasons:

- Victims may not be aware that they are victims, as in the case of fraud or some types of child abuse.
- Victims may assume that they will not be believed. It is only in recent years that children have been taken seriously as victims of sexual crime.
- Some crimes, such as soft drug offences and prostitution, appear to have no victim and consequently may not be reported by the general public as consistently as other crimes.
- Some victims may fear humiliation at the hands of the police, the courts, the media and society in general. Sue Lees (1995) refers to women's fear of the 'second rape', i.e. the courtroom ordeal of being aggressively cross-examined by defence counsel seeking to 'prove' sexual provocation by the victim, as a major reason why a substantial number of rape victims may be unwilling to report what has happened to them.
- Some victims, especially members of minority cultures or persecuted groups, such as ethnic minorities and asylum-seekers, may distrust the police and therefore fail to report crimes. In some cases there may be grounds for fearing that the police will not take offences seriously. For example, racial violence was only made illegal in its own right in 1998.

- There is evidence that changes in police attitudes towards rape victims in the 1980s, reflected in sensitivity training for police officers and the introduction of rape suites, led to an artificial rise in rape statistics as more victims were willing to come forward.
- Similarly, the introduction of Childline in the 1980s allowed child victims of sexual abuse to be taken seriously. The statistics for this offence rose, but again this reflected a rise in reporting rather than a real increase in the offence.

Any attempt to improve victims' ability to recognise that a crime has been committed against them or to encourage victims to come forward may result in an artificial rather than a real increase in the official crime statistics.

Social reactions to crime — the role of the mass media and moral panics

Stanley Cohen (1972) argues that the mass media play a key role in the construction of criminal statistics because most of the information that the public (i.e. those who report crime and suspicious behaviour) get about crime comes from television and newspapers, particularly tabloid newspapers. Consequently, how we see crime and 'typical' potential criminals may be shaped by media reporting. The official criminal statistics may be 'amplified' or exaggerated by media reports as follows:

- The media take an interest in a particular social group and interpret its behaviour as 'deviant' or as 'anti-social', i.e. the group or activity is defined as newsworthy (interesting enough to sell newspapers or to attract a television audience) and is presented as a social problem.
- Moreover, the causes of the so-called problem are simplified and linked to the social anxieties of the period. In the case of mods and rockers in the 1960s, Cohen reports that their behaviour was seen as a symptom of the decline of morality, especially growing disrespect among the young for the older generation and the establishment.
- The media report on the group or activity using sensationalist language and headlines which exaggerate the threat to society posed by the group or activity. This is the essence of what Cohen calls a '**moral panic**'.
- Follow-up articles engage in a process of negatively labelling or stereotyping the social group by allocating symbolic features to its members, e.g. dress codes and types of behaviour, so that the general public can easily recognise them. Cohen refers to this as 'demonisation' — members of the so-called 'problem' group are transformed into '**folk devils**' to be feared by society.
- Some moral panics, e.g. that associated with mods and rockers in the 1960s, have involved a self-fulfilling prophecy stage, when media predictions that a 'problem' will occur again are themselves responsible for the recurrence. In the case of mods and rockers, the media predicted that further trouble would break out between the two groups at resorts during the next bank holiday, and violent conflict did indeed arise when young people converged on these resorts in response to what they had read.

- Moral entrepreneurs, such as members of parliament and newspaper editors, put pressure on the government and agencies of control, such as the police, to deal severely with the 'problem' group. In reaction to this pressure, members of the public are more aware of the so-called problem group and are therefore more willing to report 'suspicious' behaviour associated with this group, thus increasing the crime statistics.
- Media coverage may have the effect of attracting more people to the 'problem' as it becomes a symbol of resistance to the establishment. Young (1971) argues that the moral panic over cannabis smoking in the late 1960s had precisely this effect.
- The law stamps down hard on the 'problem' group by policing it more heavily. Arrests and convictions consequently rise dramatically. New laws may be introduced aimed at controlling and criminalising the group or activity in question.
- There may be a 'reaction effect', as such treatment and criminalisation lead to resistance and confrontation with the authorities and the deviant social group acquires cult status. For example, both Redhead (1992) and Thornton (1996) note that the moral panic that surrounded rave parties in the late 1980s and early 1990s had the effect of alienating young people, who confronted police officers attempting to break up their parties, resulting in mass arrests.

This process — known as a deviancy amplification spiral — results in an artificial increase in the official criminal statistics. If the media had not taken a selective interest in the so-called 'problem' activity, it is doubtful whether the activity would have been defined as deviant and it is unlikely that there would have been an escalation in its scale. In summary, then, the official criminal statistics for some juvenile crimes may simply reflect public intolerance fuelled by journalists' construction of moral panics in search of newsworthy stories.

Key concepts

moral panic; deviancy amplification; newsworthiness; demonisation; folk devils; self-fulfilling prophecy; moral entrepreneurs; reaction effect; criminalisation

Power, control and criminalisation

The police and criminalisation

It is argued that the official criminal statistics tell us more about the nature of policing in the UK than about crime and criminality. In particular, they may tell us a great deal about police administrative procedures, how police officers interact with suspects, especially those from relatively powerless social groups, and police culture.

Administrative influences
- The police exercise discretion in whether they record crime reported by the public and consequently only about 40% of reported crimes are recorded by officers.
- There have been changes in police practice over the last 20 years, especially with regard to how officers deal with rape, domestic violence and racial attacks.

Consequently, any changes in trends relating to sexual offences and violence may be artificial, reflecting not an increase in the volume of such crime but rather a greater confidence in the police.
- The 43 police forces in the UK do not operate in a standardised fashion. The official criminal statistics on cannabis use, prostitution and homosexual importuning are unreliable because some forces consistently crack down on these offences whilst others turn a blind eye to them.
- The common use of surveillance cameras in city centres and at football stadiums inevitably leads to an increase in arrests, prosecutions and convictions. The crimes involved have probably not increased, but the technology increases the detection rate and police efficiency.

Police–suspect interaction

Interpretivist sociologists argue that we need to understand that the official criminal statistics are a social construction in that they originate in interaction between police officers and suspects. They point out that:
- The interaction is not equally balanced because police officers have the power to choose to ignore an incident, to give a warning or to arrest.
- Police officers, like most members of society, are likely to operate using stereotypical assumptions or labels about what constitutes 'suspicious' or 'criminal' in terms of social types and behaviour, i.e. the decision to stop or arrest suspects may be based on whether they correspond to a stereotype.
- Studies of police officers on the beat in the UK by Smith and Gray (1980), Holdaway (1983) and others confirm that they divide society into two broad stereotypical categories, i.e. respectable and potentially criminal. If members of the public fit the criminal stereotype, they are more likely to be stopped, arrested and charged.
- There is strong evidence to suggest that racial stereotyping may be a crucial element in some police officers' interaction with black people, especially African-Caribbeans, and their decision to stop them.
- Holdaway (2000) rejects the notion that the police are racist but agrees with Lord McPherson's report into the death of Stephen Lawrence, which found that the London Metropolitan police were guilty of 'institutional racism' (i.e. unwitting prejudice, ignorance, thoughtlessness and racial stereotyping which disadvantaged minority ethnic groups) with regard to how they dealt with black people. The police initially failed to understand that Stephen Lawrence had been murdered because he was black and also assumed that all black people near the site of the killing (including Lawrence's best friend, who had witnessed the attack) were suspects rather than witnesses.
- Home Office statistics on police stop and search released in November 2002 support the notion of racial stereotyping because they reveal that black people are eight times more likely than white people to be stopped and searched. Officers in London in 2001–02 stopped 30% more African-Caribbean people and 40% more Asian people than in 2000, while the increase for white people was only 8%. Only one in ten stops led to an arrest.

- Holdaway (2002) concludes that there is still substantial evidence of the stereo-typing of ethnic minorities in the form of derogatory language, jokes and banter and the way that officers from ethnic-minority backgrounds are treated by white officers.
- In addition, Holdaway argues that racial stereotyping has led to an over-policing of black areas and to a reaction effect in the form of urban riots in London.
- It may also be the case that young people in general, males and working-class people fit a criminal stereotype and may be more likely to be the subject of police attention than older people, females and middle-class people respectively.
- Feminist criminologists argue that male officers tend to adopt paternalistic attitudes towards female offenders, who are less likely to be stopped, arrested and charged, i.e. females are less likely to be stereotyped as 'suspicious' or criminal and when found committing criminal offences are more likely to be let off with only a caution.

Police culture

Sociological studies of the occupational culture (sometimes called 'canteen culture') of the police suggest that it sustains negative views within the workforce, especially among the rank and file officers, about ethnic and other minorities. There is evidence that older and more experienced officers transmit racist attitudes to younger officers and use racist language as a matter of course in their presence. It can be difficult for younger officers to challenge such attitudes and language without being labelled as being deviant.

- Box (1987) suggests that this police culture is understandable in the context of the social origins and educational experiences of police officers because most are from white working-class backgrounds and have failed to achieve academically compared with their middle-class peers.
- Research indicates that police culture is predominantly masculine (women officers constitute less than 20% of officers) and interaction with groups, such as young men or ethnic minorities, may be compromised by a need to be seen to be tough by other officers, i.e. a cult of masculinity may exist amongst officers.
- Lambert's survey of police officers (1990) suggests that they see themselves as middle class and as having the special status of protecting the middle classes from 'inferior' groups such as the working class and ethnic minorities. In other words, the police self-identify as the 'thin blue line'.
- Other surveys of police attitudes carried out by Smith and Gray (1976) and others note that police officers tend to subscribe to conventional views and to be highly critical of those whose ideas and lifestyles are very different.
- Box's research found that many officers vote Conservative and are dependent upon the tabloid newspapers for their opinions.
- Research by Smith and Gray suggests that the mundane nature of police work may lead officers to be over-zealous in their policing in order to create excitement and interest.
- Police stereotyping of communities may stem from changes in organisational practices such as the introduction of car patrols, the decline in beat policing, and

the fact that officers are no longer recruited from the communities that they police, so they do not know these communities. If the police come into contact only with the antisocial or criminal elements within a particular community, they may regard these people as representative of whole areas. This is negative stereotyping.

Key concepts

interaction; institutional racism; stop and search; racial stereotyping; paternalism; occupational culture; canteen culture; cult of masculinity

The criminal justice system and criminalisation

The idea that everyone is equal before the law is central to the UK legal system. However, some sociologists suggest that this may be a myth. Research into the social background of magistrates and judges has raised the question of whether there is class, gender and racial bias in the system which may be partly responsible for the disproportionate number of young, black and working-class people in the official criminal statistics and the prison population.

- Research by Hood (1990) found that almost 80% of magistrates are from the professional classes I and II, while there is a marked absence of unskilled working-class, black and Asian magistrates.
- Griffiths' research into the social and educational backgrounds of the judiciary (1980) indicates that the vast majority of judges come from upper-class backgrounds. Up to 70% of them attended the top public schools and Oxbridge.
- Griffiths found that judges tend to be disproportionately male and white and aged over 60.
- Griffiths argues that these very narrow social backgrounds make it difficult for magistrates and judges to understand the situations and experiences of the working-class and black people who appear in front of them. Box's research found that magistrates and judges are more likely to see middle-class criminality as an 'accident' or as out of character and consequently treat such offenders more leniently than working-class or black offenders.
- Hood's study of 3,300 cases heard in the West Midlands Crown Courts in 1989 found that black males have a 17% greater chance of receiving a custodial sentence than white males for the same offence, and that the average length of prison sentence was longer for both blacks and Asians when they pleaded not guilty.
- Worral (1995) argues that judicial attitudes are also gender-biased. Women who conform to a 'feminine' stereotype are more likely to be treated leniently by the courts whereas women who argue their case confidently or who are interpreted as 'unfeminine' by judges may receive more severe sentences.

The state and criminalisation

The Marxist critique suggests that the capitalist state collects and constructs criminal statistics in order to serve the interests of the capitalist class that controls it. The statistics serve an ideological function — whoever has the power to collect and construct such statistics has the power to control and manipulate public opinion and concern (see pp. 18–19). This power contributes to the reproduction and maintenance of ruling-class power in the following ways:

- Box (1987) argues that the law and the criminal statistics are used to criminalise the activities of the powerless and give society the impression that the 'problem population' is the working class and ethnic-minority groups. This confirms the stereotypes that these groups are 'morally inferior' to the rest of society and 'deserve' more social controls, i.e. more policing of their areas and more laws to control their behaviour.
- These powerless groups are treated in this way because they are perceived by the powerful to be a potential threat to the existing distribution of power, wealth and privilege.
- The scapegoating of these powerless groups distracts society from the real problems of capitalist societies such as high unemployment, low wages, exploitation at work and inequalities in wealth and income, i.e. problems caused by the management of capitalism by the ruling class.
- The criminal statistics suggest to the general public that crimes committed by the powerful are a minor problem, but Box argues that such crimes are not pursued as vigorously or punished as harshly as working-class crimes.
- Box also argues that the powerful engage in anti-social activities which result in death, injury and theft for ordinary people, especially members of the working class, but these activities are often not defined as criminal because the ruling class controls the making of law. For example, Box suggests that employers' deliberate failure to maintain safe working conditions, drug manufacturers' failure to adequately test their products, misrepresentation by advertisers, price fixing, pollution etc. should all be defined as serious crimes but are not.
- Box concludes that few people are aware of the crimes of the powerful or how serious these are because society's attention is focused on the official crime statistics. The crimes of the powerful are rendered invisible.

Overall, Box argues that the official criminal statistics are not meant to tell us the truth about crime. They actually tell us very little about the real level of crime in society and do little to help us understand criminality.

The left-realist view

Left realism is sympathetic to both interpretivist and Marxist critiques of the official criminal statistics. It agrees that the media and police pay disproportionate attention to powerless social groups and that ruling-class crime is not adequately addressed by law-enforcement agencies. However, Lea and Young (1992) argue that these explanations are insufficient in explaining why working-class and black youth are more likely to turn up in the criminal statistics.

- Using data from victim surveys, Lea and Young suggest that working-class and black youth are the main perpetrators of crime in the inner cities.
- The types of crime committed by these groups — violence, mugging, burglary etc. — are those that ordinary people fear and these fears are justified in inner-city areas.

- The victims of these crimes are often working-class, black and female.
- In the UK and other democracies ordinary people do not live in fear of state or corporate crime. Inner-city crime, on the other hand, has real consequences, i.e. people in affected communities are afraid to go out after dark.
- Victim surveys indicate that the official criminal statistics seriously underestimate certain types of crime, e.g. burglary, and overestimate others, e.g. criminal damage.
- Left realism is critical of both interpretivist and Marxist approaches for suggesting that statistics are a social construction, i.e. the product of media, police and ruling-class practices. Left realists argue that it is irresponsible of these theories not to recognise the devastating effect that everyday crime and fear of crime is having on inner-city communities.

Key concepts

capitalist state; ideological function; scapegoating; victim surveys

Patterns of victimisation

In the last 10 years, criminologists have paid considerable attention to the victims of crime. A number of sociological approaches have located the victim at the centre of the debate about law and order.

- Sociologists working for the Home Office have been responsible for the British Crime Survey, a type of victim survey which is often used in conjunction with the official criminal statistics to produce a more rounded picture of crime in the UK. Results from this survey have been used by right realists (see pp. 44–47) to support their case that victims can play a major role in crime prevention.
- Left realists such as Lea and Young have constructed their own victim survey, the Islington Crime Survey, to illustrate the reality of inner-city crime.
- Feminists have drawn our attention to the victimisation of women and children in the home.
- Marxist sociologists have demonstrated that we are all potentially victims of corporate and state crime (see pp. 35–38).

The British Crime Survey

Victim surveys attempt to give us a better understanding of the reality of crime than is provided by the official criminal statistics. The British Crime Survey (BCS) was started by the Home Office in 1983 and is now conducted annually. It involves sending a questionnaire to over 10,000 households drawn from the Postcode Address File (a sampling frame) and is designed to be as nationally representative a sample as possible in order to generalise the results to the country as a whole. It is used by the government to help devise policies on crime.

By asking respondents in this sample to report all crimes of which they have been victims, and whether or not they reported these crimes to the police, the survey aims to answer the following questions:

- How much crime is there?
- What is the gap between recorded crime and actual crime?
- For each category of crime, how likely is it to be reported?
- Why are some crimes not reported?
- What sort of people are most likely to be victims of crime?
- What is the relationship between people's fear of crime and the reality?

Over the years, the British Crime Survey has reached the following conclusions:
- Only around one in four crimes is reported to the police.
- Theft of motor vehicles is most likely to be reported (98%), but the vast majority of other crimes have a reporting rate of less than 50%. Vandalism is the most under-reported crime.
- Only approximately 54% of reported crime is recorded by the police, so the number of crimes committed is much higher than police figures suggest.
- Most victims report property crime rather than violent crime. About 62% of all reported offences involve theft.
- Only about a quarter of the samples report being affected by crime 'very much' or 'quite a lot'. Most victims are not greatly affected by offences committed against them.
- Robbery and wounding are regarded as the most traumatic crimes against the person whilst burglary is the most traumatic property crime — the invasion of privacy is the most upsetting effect for many victims, especially women.
- Many respondents have experienced 'repeat victimisation', e.g. being burgled on a number of successive occasions or suffering regular domestic violence over a period of time. Repeat victimisation can have severe emotional effects in terms of fear of crime.
- Women worry more about all crimes except vehicle crime — nearly one-third worry about the possibility of being raped and a third of elderly women say that they feel very unsafe out alone after dark.
- Those who fear violent crime the most (the elderly and women) are least likely to be victims of it, while those who are least afraid (young men) are most likely to be victims of crime.
- The first British Crime Survey in 1983 concluded that fear of serious crime is out of proportion to its reality. It estimated that the average person is likely to be burgled once every 40 years, assaulted once every 100 years, robbed once every 500 years, and have their car stolen once every 60 years.
- The most common reason for not reporting crime is that it is 'too trivial'. This is followed by a lack of confidence in the police's ability to clear up crime.

Evaluation

+ It is claimed that the British Crime Survey is more valid than the official criminal statistics because it uncovers the dark figure of crime, i.e. crimes not reported to the police and therefore not recorded.
− Like most surveys, the BCS uses standard classifications of crime, i.e. crimes commonly committed against the general public by individuals, and consequently omits business crime.

- It is based on households only — it does not examine institutional victims.
- It has generally failed to ask questions about serious crimes such as rape.
- It does not record 'victimless' crimes such as prostitution, drug-taking etc.
- It relies on people's memories, which may be unreliable.
- There is a danger of respondents exaggerating and/or telescoping incidents, i.e. moving them forwards and backwards in time.
- People are often unaware that they are victims — especially of crimes committed by the powerful, e.g. corporate crime.
- The survey may be influenced by ideological concerns, e.g. to reassure us that the likelihood of being a victim of crime in the UK is very slight, and consequently its objectivity may be questionable.
- Ellingworth (1995) argues that the samples used by the BCS are not representative of the national population because owner-occupiers and 16–24 year-olds are generally over-represented while the unemployed are under-represented.
- The BCS response rate in urban areas with high levels of crime is not as high as that in rural areas with low levels of crime.
- As a national study, the BCS does not trace the way in which crime is concentrated in inner-city areas because it focuses on national trends.
- The methodology of the BCS has been questioned. It is argued that questionnaires are an impersonal method of gathering private and personal information about being a victim of crime and may result in low response rates or incomplete accounts of distressing experiences.
- Pilkington (1996) notes that the BCS distorts the meaning of the numbers. Offences against the person may constitute a relatively small proportion of recorded offences, but violent and sexual offences often have a traumatic effect upon victims and their seriousness is evident by the number and length of prison sentences they warrant, i.e. over 40% of prisoners are serving time for violent or sexual crime.

Other victim surveys

Sociologists who believe that the British Crime Survey has tended to underplay the extent of crime have developed an alternative approach — a realist victimology which has focused on specific geographical regions and has attempted to produce an appraisal of being a victim of crime in urban areas. This approach also examines the influence of class, gender, ethnicity and age on being a victim of crime.

- The Merseyside Crime Survey carried out by Kinsey in 1984 found that in terms of quantity and impact of crime, the poor suffer more than the wealthy.
- The Islington Crime Survey, carried out by the left-realist sociologists Lea and Young (1986) and using sympathetic interviewing techniques, asked victims living in inner London about serious crime such as sexual assault, domestic violence and racial attack. They found that a full third of all households had been touched by serious crime in the previous 12 months.
- The Islington Crime Survey found that crime shaped people's lives to a consider-able degree. A quarter of all people always avoided going out after dark because of fear of crime and 28% felt unsafe in their own homes.

- Realist surveys have found that fear of crime is highest among low-income groups, which reflects the fact that they are most at risk from crime. The greater fears of the elderly and the poor may also reflect the greater economic and emotional impact that crime has on these groups.
- Women in the Islington Crime Survey experienced what was effectively a curfew on their activities — over half the women never went out after dark because of their fear of crime. Zedner (1992) notes that this fear was realistic in the context of this urban area and rational when the extent of unreported rape is taken into account.
- Young and Lea criticise the BCS for its focus on the 'average person' by pointing out that inner-city residents are not 'average' in terms of their experience of crime. It is realistic to worry about being burgled when the incidence of burglary in inner London is five times the national average.
- Young and Lea are critical of the methods of the BCS with regard to uncovering violent and sexual crime because women in particular may be reluctant to admit that they have been victims in a questionnaire. The Islington survey, in contrast, used carefully trained and sympathetic female researchers.

Key concepts

realist victimology; fear of crime

Feminist victim surveys

- Hanmer and Saunders used sympathetic and well-trained female interviewers to carry out a series of unstructured interviews with women living in one randomly selected street in Leeds during the 1980s. They found that 20% of these women had been sexually assaulted but had not reported the crime against them.
- A number of studies have focused on women as victims of violence in their own homes, and as a result of these studies, it is now recognised that the home is a 'major site of violence' (Croall 1998).
- Stanko carried out a snapshot survey based on all reports to police services, Victim Support, Women's Aid and Refuge and Relate on Thursday, 28 September 2000 and found that every second during the 24-hour period a woman called the police for protection from her partner.
- Stanko's research, based upon police reports and the British Crime Survey, found that a woman was killed in England and Wales by her current or former partner every 3 days in 2001, that a quarter of all violent crime in London was domestic, that there are 570,000 cases of domestic violence in the UK every year and that an incident of domestic violence occurs in the UK every 6 to 20 seconds.
- Walklate (1998) argues that many female victims of domestic violence are unable to leave their partners because of the gendered power relationships that shape and govern women's lives, i.e. they are less likely to have economic resources and therefore potential independence, they have nowhere else to go (the number of refuges in the UK is in decline), they often blame themselves, and threats of further violence and losing their children undermine their confidence.

- Kelly's research (1988) into 'survivors' of domestic violence found that many women were undermined by verbal abuse as well as physical violence.
- Past sociological research, e.g. Dobash and Dobash (1974), uncovered evidence of institutional apathy about domestic violence on the part of police forces and the government. However, the current Labour government has instructed all police forces and the courts that such violence is no longer to be tolerated and all reported crimes must be dealt with seriously.

Sociological explanations of crime and deviance

Structuralist theories

Structuralist theories generally locate the causes of crime in the ways that societies are organised or structured. These positivist theories tend to suggest that there are social forces bearing down on some individuals which make them more likely than others to commit crime and delinquency. Traditionally, the theories which have taken a structuralist line have been functionalist, subculturalist and Marxist. They have been challenged in recent years by interpretivist theories of crime and deviance which suggest that structuralist theories are overdeterministic, i.e. they neglect the capacity of people to make choices about their behaviour and therefore to resist structural influences.

Functionalist explanations

The key functionalist thinker about crime was Robert Merton. His theory of crime attempted to explain the high levels of crime committed by those in the USA in the post-Depression period of the 1930s at the bottom of the socioeconomic hierarchy (i.e. the poor, the working class, African-Americans). Merton (1938) argued that the source of crime lay in the relationship between the culture and the social structure of American society.

- The culture of American society was, according to Merton, based on the American Dream, a package of aspirations and goals deeply embedded in individuals' cultural lives. Merton assumed that the population of the USA shared similar values (i.e. there was a value consensus) in its belief that the USA was an open society in which hard work would be rewarded with material success regardless of socio-economic and ethnic background.
- This cultural goal was transmitted via education and the mass media, especially advertising, which strongly encouraged the acquisition of material goods, i.e. consumerism.

content guidance

- Merton argued that the social structure in this context was made up of the means by which people can seek to achieve the American Dream, i.e. education and employment.
- In a healthy society, Merton argued, there would be a symmetry between the cultural goals that people shared and the institutionalised means of achieving the goals, but if there was a mismatch or strain between people's pursuit of the goals and access to the means (i.e. if people underachieved in education or ended up in dead-end jobs or unemployed), they experienced blocked opportunities and a sense of 'anomie' — they felt alienated and frustrated by the system and this created a moral dilemma, i.e. should they commit crime to achieve their goals?

Merton therefore argued that crime was inversely related to social status. Those at the bottom of society were most likely to subscribe to the goals of material success and less likely to succeed in terms of access to the means. However, Merton argued that individuals could respond to this tension in a number of ways, depending both on their attitudes and on their acceptance or rejection of the goals and the means of achieving them.

- **Conformity** — the mass of the population coped with their disappointment by accepting their lot. They continued to do their best and make the most of what society offered them. In other words, they continued to dream about the goal of material success and conform to the accepted means of achieving that goal, i.e. by working hard.
- **Innovation** — some people rejected the conventional means of acquiring wealth and adopted non-conventional and illegal means, i.e. they turned to crime.
- **Ritualism** — this describes the attitude of people who lost sight of the goals but plodded on in meaningless jobs, working hard but never really thinking about what they were trying to achieve.
- **Retreatism** — a small number of people simply dropped out of conventional society and therefore rejected both the goals and the means, e.g. the drug addicts, the vagrants and those who committed suicide.
- **Rebellion** — a few might rebel and seek to replace the shared goals with alternative, often opposing goals and values. They set about achieving them by revolutionary means, e.g. via terrorism.

In conclusion, Merton explained crime committed by the poor and the working classes as a reaction to the social organisation of capitalist societies. Paradoxically he saw crime, a deviant and non-conformist activity, as caused by conformity to the dominant value system. The criminal, therefore, was not that dissimilar to the law-abiding citizen. Both were shaped by the same desires and goals, i.e. to achieve material success.

Evaluation

- The extent to which there is consensus in modern societies about goals has been questioned. Surveys indicate that the poor do not believe that they will achieve material success on a par with other social groups.
- Do all social groups aim for material success? There are people whose first goal is altruism — to help others less fortunate than themselves.

- Merton's theory explains utilitarian crime, i.e. crimes in which the end result is a material or financial benefit, but does not explain crimes of violence.
- It also fails to explain collective forms of crime such as those committed by juveniles in gangs, e.g. vandalism, territorial violence. This type of crime is not motivated by material goals.
- Merton explains why people with low social status commit crime but fails to acknowledge that the middle classes, who are educationally successful and have access to professional and managerial careers, commit white-collar and corporate crime. Surely these types of crime arise out of access to opportunities rather than any blocking of them?
- Merton's theory is contradictory. It strongly implies that people are passive victims of their circumstances. It also implies that they choose certain paths, although Merton does not explain why an individual chooses one particular form of deviant adaptation rather than another.
- Merton does not deal adequately with the issue of power. He fails to ask who benefits from the capitalist system and especially the laws that underpin it. For example, Taylor (1971) describes Merton's image of society as being like a giant fruit machine — the pay-outs are rigged but the conformists kid themselves into thinking it is fair. The innovators try to rig the machine to their advantage, the ritualists just blindly play on, not even noticing, or caring, whether they have won, the retreatists just ignore it, and the rebels smash it up and replace it with a better model. However, Taylor argues that Merton never tells us who designed the rules, who takes the profits from the game and who put the machine there in the first place.
+ Anomie is an influential concept and is implied in explanations that link crime to social and economic disadvantage, especially the idea that property crime rises in periods of recession.
+ Sumner (1994) claims that Merton uncovered the main cause of crime in modern societies, i.e. the alienation caused by disillusion with the impossible goals set by capitalism.

Key concepts

structuralist; interpretivist; overdeterministic; American Dream; material success; value consensus; cultural goals, institutionalised means; strain; anomie; conformity; innovation; ritualism; retreatism; rebellion

Subcultural explanations for youth crime

American subcultural theory emerged in the 1950s and is heavily influenced by Merton's functionalist theory of crime. It tends to focus on explaining why young working-class people commit crime, i.e. juvenile delinquency. It particularly focuses on that aspect of youth crime, i.e. gang violence, joyriding and gang warfare, which seems to be malicious in character and therefore not linked to material or financial goals. In addition, while Merton focused on deviance as an individual response to anomie, subcultural theory focuses on delinquency as a collective or subcultural response.

A subculture is a culture that exists, as the name implies, underneath the main or dominant culture of a society. It follows, therefore, that members of subcultures will have different norms, attitudes, values and beliefs from others, and because these are different from those shared by most members of a society, it follows that they might be regarded as deviant.

- Cohen (1955) starts from the observation that a central goal for everybody is the pursuit of status — a feeling of self-worth in the eyes of others as well as oneself. This is especially important for young people because material success is realistically out of their reach.
- He goes on to argue that lower-working-class boys are inadequately socialised into the 'correct' norms and values needed for both success in education and conformity to social rules because of deficiencies in their culture.
- This cultural weakness leads to lower-working-class boys being consigned to educational and occupational failure, and consequently society accords them little value and status.
- Such boys therefore have low self-esteem and experience status frustration, i.e. they feel alienated and angry at their low status in the eyes of 'respectable' society, such as teachers and employers.
- They solve this problem by developing a subculture which celebrates toughness and masculinity, and which reverses the norms and values of the dominant culture, turning upside down what is normally regarded as 'good' and bad' and awarding status on the basis of anti-social or anti-school behaviour, i.e. juvenile delinquency.

In conclusion, Cohen blames crime committed by working-class youth on both working-class culture and society. He argues that working-class parents and culture should take most of the blame because working-class boys are not taught to value education. However, he acknowledges that society should take some responsibility because it denies these youths any form of status or sense of value.

Evaluation

- It is not clear that working-class youth subscribe to the consensus in terms of wanting status through education or jobs. The lads in Paul Willis's study 'Learning to labour' (1977) did not share the same goals as conformist youth — they actually defined educational failure as success because they wanted jobs in the local car factory.
- There is little research evidence that subcultures exist or that juvenile delinquency is motivated by status frustration.
- If subcultures do exist, they are temporary phenomena. Most delinquents settle down to a life of conformity.
- Most working-class boys conform even when they leave education with few or no qualifications.
- Cohen seems to imply that lack of status will result in deviant or delinquent activity, but there may be other legitimate ways of gaining status, e.g. through sport and perhaps even through conformity.
- Cohen ignores working-class girls.

– Cohen generalises about working-class parents and culture. For example, can we really say that all working-class parents do not value education? Might some fault lie with the education system and teachers who may favour middle-class students?

Walter Miller (1958) rejects Cohen's argument that lower-working-class lads develop a distinct set of values that are opposed to the dominant culture. Rather, Miller argues that juvenile delinquency results from an extension and exaggeration of lower-working-class subcultural values.

- Miller argues that working-class values are the product of the type of work performed by manual workers, e.g. on factory assembly lines, which is routine, boring and those who do it lack power and autonomy.
- The experience of this type of work has led to working-class male culture developing a series of 'focal concerns' to compensate for the boredom of work by giving meaning to life outside it.

Examples of focal concerns include:
- an acceptance that violence is a part of life and you need to be able to look after yourself
- a heightened sense of masculinity or manliness, e.g. being tough, being able to 'hold your drink', 'getting loaded', womanising etc.
- smartness, i.e. looking good and feeling 'sharp'
- excitement, i.e. looking for 'kicks', a desire for fun etc.
- fatalism, i.e. an acceptance of fate, that nothing much can be done with their lives
- autonomy, i.e. an attitude that says 'nobody will push me around', especially people in authority, for example the police and schoolteachers

In conclusion, Miller attributes crime committed by the working classes, especially young working-class males, to the inherently deviant nature of working-class culture.

The British experience
- Downes, in a study of delinquent youth in London in 1966, found that they did not experience 'status frustration' because they had never expected to succeed in education.
- Their delinquency was motivated by what Downes called 'leisure values' — seeking fun and alleviating boredom — rather than being a product of oppositional subcultural values.
- Marxist analyses of British deviant youth subcultures such as teddy boys, mods, rockers, skinheads and punks have concluded that their value systems and behaviour were part of a symbolic attempt to challenge the authority and power (i.e. cultural hegemony) of the middle-class establishment. They used shock tactics to undermine middle-class conventions.
- Such subcultures often borrowed from their working-class parent culture in terms of dress and behaviour. For example, the territorial violence of the skinheads was thought to be the product of the frustration they felt about the decline of traditional working-class areas and lifestyles.

Evaluation

- Matza (1964), an interpretivist sociologist, argues that all subcultural theories overpredict delinquency. Most youth experience status frustration and anomie and subscribe to working-class values but do not become delinquents.
- He argues that we are all potentially deviant but only some of us actually become delinquent, while some of us drift in and out of delinquency, eventually growing out of it when we reach adulthood.
- He supports his argument that many delinquents are not committed deviants who are opposed to society's values by noting that delinquent youth use 'techniques of neutralisation' to justify their actions, i.e. they explain their actions with reference to individual justifications such as 'I didn't mean any harm' rather than with reference to commitment to a group cause.
- He argues that subcultural theories neglect the influence of the social environment and especially the distribution of power. He maintains that we all subscribe to deviant or subterranean values in that most of us crave excitement, want to be outrageous etc., but some powerless groups, such as the young working classes and black people, are more likely than the middle classes to come to the attention of the authorities and be labelled deviant.
- Marxist theories are dependent upon an analysis which is highly interpretative and possibly ideologically biased in favour of finding conflict-driven behaviour.
- Portraying delinquency as a form of political resistance romanticises delinquents as anti-heroes and plays down the devastating effect their behaviour can have on their victims. Skinheads, for example, often engage in racist attacks.
- Many of these explanations ignore females.

Key concepts

subculture; status; self-esteem; status frustration; focal concerns; fatalism; masculinity; autonomy; oppositional subcultures; cultural hegemony; techniques of neutralisation; subterranean values; political resistance

Ecological theory

During the 1920s a group of sociologists based in Chicago developed an ecological approach to the study of social life, i.e. they looked at the relationship between social actors and their urban environment. In particular, Shaw and McKay attempted to explain why crime rates were so high in cities.

- By examining the organisation of cities, they observed that most were divided into distinct neighbourhoods or zones with their own values and lifestyles.
- They paid particular attention to 'zone two', i.e. the inner city, which they referred to as the 'zone of transition', characterised by cheap housing, especially rented accommodation, high numbers of immigrants and high crime rates.
- They noted that 'relative' crime rates in the inner city were similar over a number of years even though the immigrant groups dominating the zone had changed. In other words, the high crime rates were not due to the specific cultural characteristics of particular immigrant groups.

- They concluded that the constant movement of people in and out of the area produced a state of 'social disorganisation', i.e. there was little sense of community or of duty and obligation to one's neighbours, and therefore people felt little guilt about committing crime.

In conclusion, Shaw and McKay explained crime in urban areas, i.e. that committed by the poor (the underclass), in terms of the social disorganisation of the city.

Evaluation

- Shaw and McKay's analysis of crime is tautological, i.e. it is unclear whether high crime rates are a consequence of social disorganisation or are a contributing factor to it.
- The theory may underestimate the organised nature of much crime.
- Ecological theory scapegoats whole areas and their inhabitants as potentially criminal.
- The disproportionate amount of urban crime in the criminal statistics may be due to overpolicing of urban areas.

Key concepts

ecological approach; inner city; zone of transition; social disorganisation; tautological

Marxist explanations

Traditional Marxism

The main focus of traditional Marxist theories of crime and deviance is that crime is an inevitable product of capitalism and the class inequality that this economic system generates. This theory aims to explain why crime seems to be a working-class phenomenon. Moreover, it argues that middle-class crime, in the form of white-collar crime, corporate crime and state crime, is underpoliced, underpunished and consequently underestimated.

- Marxists argue that capitalism as an economic system is characterised by an exploitative and unequal relationship between a ruling minority (i.e. a capitalist class or bourgeoisie) which controls the means of production and monopolises wealth, and a powerless majority (i.e. a working class or proletariat) whose only resource, i.e. its labour-power, is exploited by the bourgeois minority.
- Gordon (1976) argues that capitalism is characterised by class inequalities in the distribution of wealth and income, poverty, unemployment, homelessness etc. Much working-class crime is a realistic response to these aspects of class inequality.
- Gordon argues that the ideology (i.e. dominant ideas) of capitalism encourages criminal behaviour in all social classes. Values such as competition, materialism/consumerism, individualism, etc. result in self-seeking, greedy individuals rather than altruistic and community-orientated individuals willing to pursue common goals.
- The hierarchical nature of capitalism and inequalities in wealth and income may encourage non-economic crimes such as violence, sex crime, child abuse, drug

crime and vandalism because those at the bottom of the socioeconomic ladder may harbour strong feelings of hostility, envy, frustration and failure.

- Lack of job satisfaction and power at work may result in alienation for some workers, who may attempt to compensate for this by exercising power in the sexual and domestic spheres of their lives through crimes such as rape and domestic violence.

Marxists like Gordon argue that, considering the nature of capitalism, we should not be asking 'Why do the working classes commit crime?' but instead 'Why don't they commit more crime?' Other Marxists such as Althusser have attempted to answer this question. Althusser (1969) argues that the law is an ideological state apparatus which functions in the interests of the capitalist class to maintain and legitimate class inequality. This theme is explored in a number of ways by Marxist writers.

- Mannheim argues that the law is mainly concerned with protecting the major priorities of capitalism, i.e. wealth, private property and profit.
- Marxists note that laws have been passed which seem to benefit the working classes, e.g. trade union rights, health and safety, equal opportunities for women and ethnic minorities, but these are weakly enforced or they are later repealed or modified to suit the interests of the ruling class.
- Box argues that the ruling class has the power to prevent laws being passed which are not in its interest, such as legislation criminalising breaches of health and safety legislation which result in the death of workers.
- Marxists point out that law enforcement is selective and favours the rich and powerful, e.g. social security fraud inevitably attracts prosecution yet tax fraud very rarely gets to court.

Key concepts
bourgeoisie; proletariat; exploitation; ideology; ideological state apparatus

White-collar and corporate crime
Marxist sociologists argue that more attention needs to be paid by law-enforcement agencies to white-collar and corporate crime. Croall (1998) defines white-collar crime as crime committed in the course of legitimate employment involving the abuse of an occupational role. She includes fraud, accounting offences, tax evasion, insider dealing and computer crime in her definition.

- Croall notes that it is usually those at the top of the occupational hierarchy who have more opportunities to make large sums of money from these types of crime.
- She also notes that companies themselves commit crimes by failing to comply with standards of health, safety or quality laid down by the law.
- Corporate crime can have extremely serious effects. It may result in the deaths of workers and consumers or serious long-term debilitating illness because of exposure to dangerous chemicals and substances (e.g. asbestos), pollution and radiation. Every year approximately 500 workers die in the workplace, and the Health and Safety Executive has estimated that as many as two out of three fatal accidents are due to employer violation of safety legislation.

- Croall also notes the globalisation of corporate crime, meaning that Western companies may 'dump' on the developing world products such as medicines, contraceptives, high-tar cigarettes and insecticides which are banned in the West because of stringent health laws.

However, Croall notes that despite the high economic and personal costs of white-collar and corporate crime, it is not regarded as a serious problem by the general public. This may be because:

- these offences are often invisible — as Croall notes, they leave 'no blood on the streets' and we do not fear going out at night because of this type of crime
- many are very complex, involving the abuse of technical, financial or scientific knowledge which is often beyond the understanding of the 'person in the street'
- responsibility is often delegated in companies, so it can be difficult to decide where blame lies
- victimisation tends to be indirect — offenders and victims rarely come face to face, and people often don't realise they have been victims of these types of crime
- laws which aim to prevent these types of crime are often ambiguous — Croall notes that there is often a very fine line between what are acceptable and unacceptable business practices
- some white-collar crime involves moral ambiguity, e.g. many people regard tax evasion as morally acceptable and are happy to tolerate it
- enforcement of laws against white-collar and corporate crime is partly in the hands of civil agencies such as Trading Standards and the Health and Safety Executive — these organisations and the police lack the financial resources and personnel to conduct lengthy investigations and pursue complex and expensive cases
- many offences are difficult to prove in court, being too complex for juries to under-stand — and the cost of such trials can be prohibitive

Croall concludes that for all these reasons white-collar crime, which is mainly carried out by members of the middle and upper classes, is rarely reported, detected or prose-cuted. Consequently, the official criminal statistics are not a true reflection of the social character or extent of crime. For example, in 1985 the total cost of fraud reported to fraud squads amounted to £2,113 million — twice the cost of theft, burglary and robbery in the same year.

- Croall concludes that white-collar crime is not socially constructed as crime because as a society we interpret it as less threatening, and therefore as less of a problem, than the types of crimes committed by the working classes and other powerless social groups.
- Box argues that the problem of corporate crime is much more serious than we realise because the powerful people who control companies also define what counts as crime. Morally questionable activities which result in the death or injury of the less powerful are often not covered by the law.

State and political crime

What is defined as 'political' or 'legitimate' violence is the subject of fierce debate. It is often an ideological construct — for example, some violence defined as 'terrorism' is difficult to distinguish from violence that comes under the heading of 'freedom fighting'. Nelson Mandela was described by Margaret Thatcher as a terrorist but he is now respected worldwide as a statesman. Croall points out that 'war crimes' are also problematic. The Holocaust was seen as a war crime, but the dropping of atom bombs on the Japanese cities of Hiroshima and Nagasaki was defined by the West as 'necessary'.

- Chambliss (1995) defines state-organised crime as acts defined by international law as criminal and committed by state officials as representatives of the state. These include assassination, selling arms to countries who use them against their own people or to repress less powerful states, and supporting terrorist activities against elected governments.

Evaluation

- It is difficult to identify specific individuals with responsibility for making key executive decisions to commit acts of state or political crime.
- It may be difficult to ascertain whether these acts were committed with criminal intent or in the national interest.
- It may be necessary to go beyond the limits of the law in defeating terrorism.

- Measuring the extent of state and political 'crimes' is extremely difficult. They are often carried out by the most secret agencies of the state; they are often invisible; governments have more power and resources than most to cover up such activities and can actually control the flow of information and especially media content by issuing legal instructions which prevent the publication of materials in the 'public interest'.
- Amnesty International claims that state crime is far more significant than conventional crime because state-sponsored genocide and mass political killings have claimed millions of victims worldwide. Think, for example, of the millions killed in the USSR by Stalin, the disappearance of left-wing political opponents in countries such as Argentina, Chile and Brazil, and 'ethnic cleansing' in Bosnia.
- Even the British state has been accused of state murder. The so-called 'shoot to kill' policy in Northern Ireland, the Bloody Sunday killings of 13 people in Londonderry after a civil rights march in 1972, and the killings of three unarmed IRA members in Gibraltar by the SAS in 1988 are examples of alleged state murders.
- Many states also practise torture — the 'ultimate form of individualised terror' according to McLaughlin (1996). There is evidence that the British Army has used it in Northern Ireland and Kenya.
- Another area of concern has been the activities of state agencies such as the police and prisons. There have been significant numbers of questionable deaths in police custody and suicides in prison which, according to Croall, raise important issues about the standard of state care.
- There have also been concerns about shootings by the police. A number of recent victims were not dangerous criminals but 'innocent' victims of mistaken identity or intent.

- Recently the public accountability of politicians has been called into question after allegations of sleaze. Despite the high-profile imprisonments of Jeffrey Archer and Jonathan Aitken, legal action is rarely taken against political corruption — the resignation of the politicians concerned is often seen as sufficient punishment.

Key concepts

white-collar crime; corporate crime; the globalisation of crime; moral ambiguity; state crime; political crime; terrorism; genocide; ethnic cleansing

The new criminology

The neo-Marxist approach associated with the 'new criminology' of Taylor, Walton and Young (1973) generally agrees with the traditional Marxist analysis of the relationship between crime and capitalism. However, Taylor, Walton and Young are critical of traditional Marxists such as Gordon because they see the working classes as the passive victims of capitalism who are driven to criminality by factors beyond their control, i.e. class inequality. The new criminology rejects this view and insists that the working classes and members of ethnic-minority groups interpret their experience of capitalism and its constraints and make choices about how to react. From this perspective crime has a number of characteristics:

- It is a deliberate and conscious reaction to how the powerless interpret their position within the capitalist system.
- Crime is political — a reaction of the powerless to injustice, exploitation and alienation. Crimes against property, such as theft and burglary, aim to redistribute wealth, vandalism is a symbolic attack on society's obsession with property, and drug use is a rejection of or expression of contempt for the material values of capitalism.
- Criminals are not the passive victims of capitalism — they are actively struggling to alter capitalism and to change society for the better.
- The ruling class is aware of the revolutionary potential of working-class crime and has taken steps to control it. State bodies, such as the police, target working-class areas, while the state has introduced 'repressive' laws such as the Criminal Justice Acts to control the 'problem' population.

Marxist moral panic theory

Hall's Marxist theory of moral panics (1978) is an important contribution to the debate about state control of powerless groups such as the working classes and members of ethnic-minority groups. He argues that:

- In the early 1970s, British capitalism experienced a 'crisis of hegemony', i.e. the cultural domination of the ruling class, and especially their right to govern, was challenged by economic recession, rapidly rising unemployment, inflation and industrial action.
- Representatives of the working classes, such as trade unions, blamed these problems on the mismanagement of capitalism by the ruling class. Agents of the ruling class considered that such open criticism of capitalism encouraged political instability.

- The mass media colluded with the state and its agents, such as the police, to create a moral panic around the criminal offence of 'mugging' (an American term for purse- or wallet-snatching) — sensationalist news stories in the tabloid press based on information fed to them by the police demonised young black people as muggers.
- Such imagery had the effect of labelling all young African-Caribbeans as criminals and a potential threat to white people, and served the ideological purpose of turning the white working class against the black working class.
- This classic 'divide and rule' strategy diverted attention away from the mismanagement of capitalism, and the subsequent demands from the media and general public for the increased policing of black communities restored ruling-class hegemony, i.e. domination.

John Muncie (1993) notes that Marxists see moral panics as part of a capitalist legitimising process identifying 'enemies within'. The groups defined as criminal are usually working class in origin and engaged in forms of symbolic resistance or rebellion to a ruling-class hegemony (i.e. cultural dominance). The consequences of the moral panic are censure and control.

Evaluation

- Most victims of working-class crime and black crime are themselves working class and black, rather than people who benefit from the organisation of the capitalist system.
- Crimes such as murder, rape and child abuse rarely have a political motive.
- It is difficult to put into operation, and therefore accurately measure, the influence of Marxist concepts such as the 'crisis of hegemony' or 'divide and rule'.
- It is difficult, if not impossible, to uncover evidence of collusion between the ruling class, the police and the media in the deliberate creation of moral panics to act as political diversions.
- Left realists argue that to dismiss the crime highlighted by moral panics as ruling-class mystification is to ignore the real human suffering and damage caused by it.
- It is more likely that the media report these stories because crime is newsworthy (i.e. it sells newspapers). The police have long been a valuable source of information about crime for journalists.

Key concepts

new criminology; repressive laws; problem population; enemies within; crisis of hegemony; censure and control; ruling-class mystification; divide and rule

Interactionist approaches

Interactionist approaches to crime and deviance belong to the interpretivist tradition which argues that structuralist approaches are overdeterministic in their analysis of the criminal and deviant and their actions. Interpretivists argue that we need to understand that people are not pushed or pulled in particular directions by social forces beyond their control. Rather, human beings have consciousness and therefore the power to control their own destiny. Interpretivists, and particularly interactionists, are interested in looking at how criminality develops via interactions between potential deviants and the social context in which they find themselves, and how the various agencies involved in such interactions interpret and therefore construct the world around them.

Symbolic interactionism and labelling theory

Symbolic interactionism (often called 'labelling theory') explains the extent and social character of criminal and deviant behaviour with reference to how society, and especially powerful groups, react to the behaviour of less powerful groups of which they disapprove.

- Interactionists believe that 'normality' and 'deviance' are relative concepts because there is no universal or fixed agreement as to what they entail. Definitions of what is 'right' or 'wrong' behaviour differ according to historical period, culture, subculture and specific social context. For example, nudity is fine in some circumstances (in the privacy of the bathroom or bedroom and in public places such as nudist camps or particular beaches), may be tolerated and regarded as humorous at sporting events (streaking), but can be seen as a symptom of mental illness or criminality if persistently carried out in public (indecent exposure).
- Deviance is therefore a matter of interpretation — context is all-important. For instance, killing people is usually legally 'justifiable' if it is carried out by soldiers during wartime, or by police officers in the course of duty, or by the state in the form of capital punishment, but many would question whether the taking of life is warranted even in these circumstances.
- Howard Becker (1963) argues that there is no such thing as a deviant act — an act only becomes deviant when the powerful respond negatively to it and define it as criminal by constructing laws to control it.
- Deviance therefore entails two elements: a group or individual must act in a particular fashion and another group or individual with more power must label the initial activity as deviant.
- The powerful make the rules in order to define what counts as deviance and who is categorised as deviant. It is suggested that the economically powerful set the rules for the working classes, while in a patriarchal society men make the rules by which women behave, and in a racist society black people are judged and labelled according to white societal reaction.
- Usually the agents of social control, particularly the police, judiciary and mass media, work on behalf of the powerful groups to define the behaviour of less powerful groups as problematic by paying these groups disproportionate attention in terms of stop and search, arrest, prosecution and passing custodial sentences upon them. (See the sections on policing, judiciary and the official criminal statistics on pp. 19–22 for illustrations of these ideas.)
- The labelling theorist Lemert (1972) refers to the societal reaction of powerful groups as secondary deviance and argues that it is this, rather than the initial activity, that is the real problem of law and order.

Labelling theory has been particularly concerned with how the societal reaction or labelling process can lead to further deviance.

- Both Becker and Lemert argue that the label 'deviant' can have negative consequences for self-esteem because it overrides all other statuses in a person's life. It becomes a 'master status' and society interprets all actions and motives in the context of the label. For example, if a person is labelled a 'sex offender', this label shapes people's reactions whatever other statuses — father, son, neighbour etc. — that person might have.
- This treatment leads to prejudice and discrimination against those who have been labelled, e.g. ex-cons may find it difficult to find legitimate employment.
- The practical consequences of treating a person as a deviant may produce a 'self-fulfilling prophecy' in that the person labelled may see himself or herself as deviant and act accordingly.
- Such labelling may also increase the chances of reoffending by isolating the individual from society and encouraging friends and family to reject them. The 'deviant' may consequently seek comfort, sympathy, normality and status in a 'subculture' of others who have been branded with a similar label.
- Such subcultures normally have distinct value systems and rules of behaviour complete with their own definitions of 'normality' and 'deviance' which may conflict with mainstream society, thus creating the potential for further contravention of society's norms and the reinforcement of negative societal reaction.

Evaluation

+ Labelling theory has shown that defining deviance is a complex process. It is often socially constructed through interaction and is frequently a matter of interpretation.
+ It illustrates quite convincingly that definitions of deviance often stem from power differences.
+ Labelling theory was the first theory to draw sociological attention to the consequences of being labelled a deviant.
- Ackers argues that labelling theory puts too much emphasis on societal reaction. He says that the act is always more important than the reaction to it. Rape, murder and child abuse are always deviant and people who commit these crimes clearly know this — they don't need a societal reaction to bring the fact to their attention.
+ Plummer points out that labelling theory's emphasis on societal reaction is valuable because many activities are defined as deviant or non-deviant depending on the audience and/or the social context in which they occur. For instance, soft drug use is acceptable to many younger people but is deemed deviant by the establishment.
- Labelling theory fails to explain the origin of deviance. It does not explain why people commit crime in the first place or why people choose to commit certain types of crime rather than others.
- Marxists argue that although labelling theory acknowledges the role of power, it does not explain the origin of that power. Marxists, of course, argue that power originates in class relationships and that labelling is an ideological process which supports the interests of the ruling class and is often used by that class socially to control the powerless.

– Left realists note that labelling theory has drawn our attention to how potential deviants interact with the media, police and judiciary, but argue that it is guilty of over-romanticising deviance and blaming agencies of social control for the appearance of the powerless in the criminal statistics. Left realism points out that these powerless groups are probably responsible for the majority of crime.

Key concepts

social context; interaction; interpretation; labelling; societal reaction; self-fulfilling prophecy; subcultural response

Moral-panic theory

This theory originated with interactionist ideas about labelling and societal reaction. The mass media, especially tabloid newspapers, are seen by interactionists as agents of societal reaction. They define on behalf of society what counts as normality and deviance. A good case study of this process was Jock Young's *The Drug-takers* which was based on a participant observation study of the relationship between the police and marijuana smokers in Notting Hill, London, over the period 1967–69. Young argues that a number of social factors were in place which resulted in a moral panic.

- A social activity, i.e. smoking dope, was an important part of the social life of the hippy subculture (along with music, politics and sex) but not the central feature of it. Dope was mainly obtained from friends who had been abroad, e.g. to Morocco, and Young argues that there were no clear-cut criminal drug-pushers selling the drug.
- The mass media took an interest in this 'social problem' because tabloid news-papers saw such stories as newsworthy, i.e. they fitted journalistic 'news values' about what sells newspapers.
- Newspapers therefore engaged in a process of negatively labelling hippies as a threat to society. The moral indignation that underpinned their sensationalist reporting about drugs and the subsequent creation of the hippy drug-using folk devil or stereo-type were fuelled by the close relationship between journalists and the police.
- Police officers saw their own value system based on the work ethic as in opposi-tion to those of hippy drug-users, who were labelled by the police as subscribing to a bohemian, hedonistic, lazy and corrupt lifestyle. The media were happy to feed off these police stereotypes about hippies, and their reporting socially constructed a fantasy picture of hippy dope-smokers as social misfits who were psychologically unstable and easy prey for wicked drug-pushers.
- Young argues that intensive police action led to hippies uniting in a sense of injus-tice. It actually created a secretive and underground culture of drug-taking with a fairly developed value system, look and lifestyle. Drug-use came to be seen by this culture as a symbol of their difference from mainstream society, as a symbol of rebellion.
- Intensive police action led to a rise in the price of marijuana as customs cracked down on hippies bringing the drug back from North Africa, and criminal gangs moved in to meet the demand as well as importing new, harder drugs such as heroin.

- Increased police activity resulted in the marijuana user and the heroin addict beginning to feel some identity as joint victims of police persecution. This increased the interaction between marijuana users and heroin addicts and consequently the likelihood of moving from marijuana to heroin.
- The official reaction hardened: the police set up specialist drug squads to target the problem (especially celebrity use of drugs, e.g. members of the Beatles and the Rolling Stones were arrested and charged) and judges passed harsher sentences.
- This ensured continuing media interest in drug-use. Arrests were reported by the media as further evidence of an 'increasing' problem and the official criminal statistics confirmed this, thus justifying further increases in police powers and harsher sentencing. In other words, deviancy amplification occurred.
- The mass media, the general public and the police had their fears and predictions about drugs confirmed by all these processes — the self-fulfilling prophecy.
- Young concludes that this moral panic resulted in a 'fantasy problem' becoming a real problem because the drug culture went underground and attracted new recruits and because a criminal subculture emerged which made available a wider range of drugs.

Ben-Yehuda (1994), using the work of Cohen and Young, notes that moral panics have five key characteristics:

- **Concern** — there is a belief, usually generated and sustained by tabloid newspapers, that a particular group or activity is somehow a threat to social order and consensus.
- **Hostility** — the media engages in a campaign which demonises members of the group as being the enemies of society.
- **Consensus** — powerful forces, such as moral entrepreneurs, are able to drum up public support for their stance, while voices of reason find it difficult to obtain a platform or are labelled as guilty by association.
- **Disproportionality** — the societal reaction, especially the media coverage and the subsequent public concern, is excessive.
- **Volatility** — moral panics tend to come in intense short bursts. As Jones (1999) notes, it is difficult to maintain hysterical antagonism for any length of time and stories soon lose their newsworthiness.

Moral panics seem to arise most often when society is undergoing a 'moral crisis', usually linked to some sort of social change or modernisation. It is interesting to note that the first moral panics about youth in the 1950s and 1960s coincided with youth as an age category becoming a distinctive consumer group with values, norms of behaviour, consumption patterns and tastes which were very different from those of the older generation. Studies of moral panics from this period suggest that the older generation was concerned that such social and economic developments were undermining both the moral order and traditional authority. The moral panics about punk rock in the late 1970s (generated by the appearance of The Sex Pistols swearing on television), new age travellers in the 1980s and dance music in the 1990s can also be seen to be linked to moral anxiety.

- Punks, with their anarchic view of the establishment (e.g. 'Anarchy in the UK') and their use of shock symbols, such as the swastika and safety pins in their noses, were regarded as particularly problematical in 1977, the year of the Queen's Silver Jubilee.
- The rave or acid house music scene was seen by the older generation, especially after the ecstasy-related death of Leah Betts, as a symbol of a drug-fuelled- or e-generation in need of stricter controls (see the work of Thornton (1996) or Redhead (1992)).

Evaluation

+ Muncie notes that moral-panic theory has drawn our attention to the power of the media in categorising normal and deviant behaviour.
+ It has given us some sociological insight into the consequences of labelling in terms of how labelled groups react to media demonisation.
+ The moral-panic thesis reminds us to question our commonsensical understanding of crime and especially the media reporting of crime.
− There has been such an explosion of moral panics in recent years (e.g. satanic child abuse, single-parent families, dangerous dogs, paedophilia) that some sociologists claim that the concept has been devalued as a sociological tool.
− Some commentators claim that moral panics do not reflect social or moral anxieties held by a majority of society's members. They are simply the product of the desire of journalists and editors to sell newspapers, and constitute a good example of how audiences are manipulated by the media for commercial purposes.
− Marxists argue that the interactionist explanation for moral panics is too vague, especially in terms of whom such panics benefit. They argue that moral panics are an ideological tool of the capitalist class aimed at diverting attention away from the crises which often beset capitalism, and at dividing and ruling sections of the working classes (see pp. 38–39).
− Left realists argue that moral panics are based in reality, i.e. the groups identified are often a very real threat to those living in inner-city areas. Moral-panic theory can be harmful if it portrays crime as imagined, denying the suffering that such crime inflicts.

Key concepts

moral indignation; official reaction; fantasy problem; concern; hostility; consensus; disproportionality; volatility; moral crisis

Realist approaches

Right-realist explanations

These perspectives on crime, associated with the American sociologist W. J. Wilson (1987), became very influential on Home Office policy-making in the 1980s during the Conservatives' period in office. However, some aspects of this thinking have also been adopted by the Labour government which came to power in 1997. A number of assumptions can be identified in this type of thinking about crime:

content guidance

- Human beings are naturally selfish, individualistic and greedy, and are therefore 'naturally' inclined towards criminal behaviour if it can further their interests.
- Rehabilitation of criminals is a 'soft' option — the rate of reoffending suggests it does not work — so punishment and deterrence should be the primary aims of the justice system.
- Policies aimed at tackling crime by removing social and economic inequalities associated with poverty and unemployment have failed because they misunderstand the origins of crime. Wilson notes that the great Depression in the USA in the 1930s did not result in a parallel rise in crime.
- The police have generally failed in their attempts to prevent and reduce crime. Clear-up rates have not significantly improved and nor have crime rates gone down, despite a substantial rise in police recruitment and new technology.
- Informal controls imposed by neighbours, family and peer groups, i.e. community controls, are breaking down. The welfare state has undermined our sense of obligation to support each other and the notion of community responsibility has declined.

This rather gloomy picture of human nature and crime has led to the development of right-realist theories which stress that sociologists should abandon attempts to explain the causes of crime and instead focus on finding practical solutions to slow down the growth of crime.

Control theory

Control theory is concerned with finding practical solutions to the crime problem. Hirschi (1969), for example, argues that the sociological focus should no longer be on why people commit crime but on why more people do not. He argues that most crime is 'opportunistic' — anyone would commit it if the situation was right and he or she stood little chance of being caught. However, people are rational in their actions and choices: they weigh up the 'costs' and 'benefits' of their behaviour and generally decide that they have too much at stake to risk getting involved in criminal activity. Four controls operate to make most people keep their actions within the bounds of the law:

- **attachment** — commitment to family relationships which might be threatened by involvement in criminality
- **commitment** — years invested in education, building up a career or business, buying a house and acquiring a reputation — all these may be lost if a person is involved in crime
- **involvement** — people may be actively involved in community life as volunteers, magistrates, parent governors at local schools etc. — aspects of their lives that would be jeopardised by criminal activity
- **belief** — many people have been brought up to have strong beliefs in rules, discipline and respect for others and the law

Hirschi's theory is quite useful in explaining why younger people may turn to crime: they have less to lose. It is as people get older that they start to be influenced by the four controls described above.

Underclass theory

This theory, associated with Murray, can be linked to Hirschi's theory. Murray (1990) suggests that in both the USA and the UK there exists a distinct lower-class subculture, below the working class, which subscribes to deviant and criminal values rather than mainstream values, and transmits this deficient culture from generation to generation. This particular subculture lacks the distinctive controls that Hirschi described, so when it comes to crime, the benefits clearly outweigh the costs. We can see this when we examine Murray's description of the features of the underclass:

- People belonging to this subculture are likely to be long-term unemployed because they are workshy, i.e. they choose not to work despite work being available to them.
- They prefer to be welfare-dependent, i.e. to live off state benefits.
- They supplement their income by being involved in criminality and the black economy.
- The subculture is hostile towards the police and authority in general.
- The subculture is generally lacking in moral values and especially commitment to marriage and family life. A large percentage of underclass children are brought up by single mothers who, as this theory goes, are irresponsible parents.

This alleged underclass has been seen by politicians in recent years as the main cause of crime in inner-city areas and on council estates.

New-right/control theory solutions to crime

Conservative control thinkers believe that the best way to reduce crime is not to change the criminal but to take practical measures to reduce opportunity and make the situation more difficult for the criminal, i.e. to make sure that the costs of crime clearly outweigh the benefits. A number of solutions have been suggested:

- Wilson puts stress on the certainty of capture to increase the risks of criminal behaviour. He believes in 'zero tolerance' policing, i.e. the police should keep the streets clear of all deviant elements, especially those which threaten to undermine or threaten the sense of community within neighbourhoods.
- van der Haag (1996) argues for tougher laws to deter people from crime, especially the poor. The concepts of 'three strikes and you're out' and of punishment for parents who do not control their children concur with this view.
- Criminologists based at the Home Office have devised policies that increase the risk of being caught, including 'target hardening' or 'designing out crime' in which householders and car-owners are encouraged to invest in alarms, locks, property-marking etc., and there is increased surveillance through the use of CCTV and Neighbourhood Watch schemes.

Evaluation

- Some Weberian sociologists (notably Rex and Tomlinson 1990) agree that an underclass exists, but disagree that this is a deviant subculture responsible for its own situation and devoted to criminal behaviour. Rather, survey evidence suggests that the poor subscribe to mainstream values and that their poverty is caused by factors beyond their control such as global recession or government policies.

- Murray is criticised by labelling theorists for scapegoating the poor and long-term unemployed and encouraging the state to engage in the negative surveillance of this social grouping.
- There is no convincing empirical evidence that the underclass as a distinct subculture with distinctive values and behaviour actually exists.
- Cohen (1996) argues that new-right thinking leads to class inequalities in victimisation. The rich live in 'paranoid fortress communities' guarded by technology and private security forces, thus displacing crime to poorer and less protected areas.
- Marxists argue that we are not naturally greedy — rather, greed is socially constructed by the ideologies of consumerism and materialism which are aspects of capitalist ideology.

Key concepts

rehabilitation; deterrence; community responsibility; control theory; opportunistic crime; costs and benefits; attachment; commitment; involvement; belief; underclass; welfare dependency; zero tolerance; 'three strikes and you're out'; target hardening; designing out crime

Left-realist explanations

Left realists, such as Lea and Young (see p. 24), aim to explain street crime in urban areas. Their victim survey of inner-city Islington suggested that working-class and black people, especially elderly women, had a realistic fear of street crime.
- Young and Lea argue that despite evidence of police institutional racism, the official criminal statistics are probably largely correct in their conclusions that the working classes and, in some areas of London, African-Caribbeans, do commit most crime.
- They agree that white-collar and corporate crime is underdetected and therefore underpunished, but point out that it does not impact negatively on ordinary people's lives in the same way as mugging or burglary.
- They believe that it is too simplistic to argue that poverty is responsible for crime in the inner city, and naïve to suggest that working-class criminals are political in their motives and aim of challenging the foundations of capitalism.

Lea and Young's explanation of why working-class and African-Caribbean people commit crime revolves around three key concepts:
- Crime is partly caused by feelings of 'relative deprivation'. Working-class youth compares itself with middle-class youth, and African-Caribbean youth compares itself with white youth with regard to life chances and living standards, access to consumer goods, income etc., and these groups feel that they are relatively worse-off through no fault of their own. In the case of young blacks, they may feel that racism is holding them back, while young working-class people may believe that they have relatively few opportunities for advancement.
- Such groups may consequently feel marginalised (i.e. they feel they have little or no power to change their situation) and frustrated. Negative treatment by the police

and the authorities may result in further feelings of hostility and resentment which may spill over into confrontation.

- Some members of these groups (but not all) may look to form or join subcultures to help them cope with the feelings of frustration resulting from relative deprivation and marginalisation. In terms of deviant subcultural responses, working-class and black youth may be involved in criminal activities such as drug-pushing and street crimes such as mugging.

Evaluation

+ Hughes (1991) notes that left realists should be valued for the challenge they posed to radical criminology's thinking on the issues of intra-class and intra-ethnic crimes.
+ Left realism has drawn our attention to the brutalising effects of street crimes in the inner city and the fact that some theories of crime have romanticised offenders.
+ It has highlighted the effects of crime for victims — a group neglected by most theories of crime.
+ It realistically acknowledges that the police amplify the presence of some groups in the criminal statistics through the use of stop and search, but points out that policing is quite rightly focusing on those groups most likely to commit crime.
− There is no empirical evidence to support the view that young working-class or black criminals interpret their realities in the way described by Lea and Young, i.e. on the basis of feelings of relative deprivation and marginalisation. Research on the motives of offenders is required.
− Lea and Young do not really explain why the majority of working-class and African-Caribbean youth does not turn to crime.
− Left realism only focuses on collective or subcultural criminal responses and does not explain crimes such as burglary, which are committed by individuals rather than gangs.
− It focuses exclusively on street crime and largely ignores other serious crimes such as fraud.
− It fails to account for opportunist crime committed by adults.

Key concepts

relative deprivation; marginalisation; subcultures; intra-class crime; intra-ethnic crime

Feminist approaches

Crime and gender

The official criminal statistics tend to show that women commit less crime than men. Approximately 80% of those convicted of serious crimes are men. Consequently, there are only approximately 2,000 women in prison, accounting for about 4% of the total prison population. Analysis of their offences shows that there are differences in the types of crime committed by men and women: the majority of women are imprisoned for non-violent crimes (although female crimes of violence have increased in recent years and there has been an increase in the proportion of crime committed by women). These statistics have been interpreted in two broad ways. Some sociologists argue that the statistics are actually incorrect — women commit more crime than is acknowledged but they are often treated more leniently by the police and the courts, and consequently their crimes are less likely to be recorded, reported and prosecuted. Others argue that the statistics are largely correct, i.e. women do commit less crime because the feminine value system into which they are socialised means that they are less likely to subscribe to behaviour which attracts police and judicial attention.

Is female crime underestimated by the official criminal statistics?

- Pollack (1961) believed that women are naturally better at concealing crime and consequently much female crime is hidden. He saw women as being naturally deceitful and suggested that women's domestic roles provided opportunities for committing crimes that could easily be covered up, e.g. child abuse and domestic violence.

Evaluation
- These claims are based on unsubstantiated stereotypical images of women.
- Victim surveys provide little support for the view that women are committing crime and getting away with it (although male victims of domestic violence may be too embarrassed to report it).
- Research by the NSPCC has found it is overwhelmingly males who commit child abuse.

- Pollack and others have suggested that the police and the courts treat female offenders more leniently. It is suggested that police culture (which is overwhelmingly male) is 'paternalistic' and sexist. Females do not fit police stereotypes of 'suspicious' or 'criminal' behaviour and are consequently less likely to be stopped, arrested and charged.
- The idea that there is a 'chivalry factor', as it has become known, has been lent support by the fact that the police are more likely to caution females than males.
- Self-report surveys, most notably the one conducted by Campbell (1984), are often cited as evidence that females are committing more crime than is recorded.
- Steffensmeier (1995) argues that women are treated more leniently by the courts because judges are reluctant to separate women from children and regard women as less dangerous than men. It is suggested that judges also see women's motives for crimes as qualitatively different to those of men. Women are seen as acting emotionally and irrationally, whereas men's criminal actions are seen as being motivated by greed, wickedness and a natural propensity to violence.
- Allen (1995) notes how women are often given psychiatric care as an alternative to prison because the courts believe that they are more prone to emotional crisis.

- Police treatment is not consistent with the chivalry thesis. Prostitutes and rape victims have long complained about uncaring and callous treatment from police officers.
- Although women are cautioned more, this may have more to do with the less serious nature of their offences.
- There is evidence that women may be treated more harshly by the courts for certain types of crime, e.g. child abuse and murder of male partners (even if male domestic violence was involved).
- There is evidence, e.g. Shacklady-Smith (1985), that female delinquents are given custodial sentences in order to protect them from 'promiscuity'.
- Heidensohn (1996) notes that women are treated more harshly by the police and the courts when they deviate from social norms of traditional female femininity and sexuality.
- The chivalry factor does not take account of factors such as social class, ethnicity and age, i.e. working-class, black and teenage women are more likely to be treated harshly.

Reasons why women commit less crime than men

Some feminist criminologists accept that women commit less crime than men. Some, like Heidensohn and Leonard (1990), believe that we can gain insights from women's conformity to rules and the law which will help us understand why males commit crime. This especially makes sense when we realise that gender is probably the most crucial variable in predicting criminality. Surprisingly, few studies of crime have stressed this factor.

Invisible females

- Merton (1938) discussed cultural goals as though they were universal and did not consider that men and women might pursue different goals. This is surprising because women's responsibilities in the home when Merton was writing implied that they would be less likely to be concerned with material success, and this might account for their lower participation in crime.
- All types of subcultural theory have tended to focus exclusively on males. Miller (1958) concluded that working-class crime and deviance may be a natural consequence of the stress put on aspects of masculinity in that culture, e.g. toughness, drinking and risk-taking.
- Marxism has generally been gender-blind. The work of Taylor, Walton and Young (1973), for example, fails to mention women despite focusing on power relations.
- Realist theories have also failed to address aspects of women's experience. Left realism does not link the key concepts of relative deprivation/marginalisation to female experience while control theory, which has the potential to explore gender, fails to address the issue.

Double deviants

- There has been a tendency by the media and the courts to see female criminality as pathological — the product of factors such as biological and psychological abnormalities and 'women's problems' such as premenstrual tension and the menopause. Consequently, women are much more likely than men to be referred for medical and psychiatric reports in court.

• The courts often assume the sexualisation of delinquency, i.e. that delinquency is somehow the product of sexual promiscuity.

Evaluation

– Carlen argues that the idea that women are doubly deviants (i.e. physically or mentally abnormal and criminal) serves to neutralise the real causes of women's crime, i.e. their social and economic circumstances.

Differential socialisation and social controls

• Both Smart (1979) and Oakley (1973) have suggested that males are socialised into being tough and aggressive whilst females are socialised to accept passive, caring roles and consequently lack the non-conformist values associated with delinquency and crime.

• Heidensohn argues that a great deal of crime, especially violent, sexual and domestic crime, is 'gendered'. It seems that 'normal' masculine behaviour may overlap with criminal behaviour on occasion because hegemonic definitions of masculinity involve notions of control, authority and dominance which may result in violence.

• Women and girls may be subjected to stronger social controls than men in patriarchal societies. Smart (1979) notes that girls are more strictly supervised by their parents, especially in terms of activities outside the home, and have less opportunity to engage in juvenile delinquency.

• McRobbie and Garber's work (1976) concluded that the strains of adolescence were different for girls and their lives revolved around a 'bedroom culture' centred on worshipping pop stars which rarely brought them into contact with delinquency.

• Heidensohn uses aspects of control theory to note that women are controlled by their family roles as wives and mothers. The latter role, in particular, means they have little time or opportunity for illegal activity.

• In public, females are controlled by fear of acquiring a 'bad' reputation. Lees (1992) notes that girls are anxious to behave well in public and avoid being labelled as a 'slag' or as 'loose'.

Opportunities to commit crime

• Leonard notes that females are rarely in a position to commit crime because as adolescents they are more likely to be confined to the home, whereas males are more likely to spend much of their spare time with their male peers in public spaces where opportunities for delinquency might arise.

• In adulthood, females may be constrained by their role as mother. It is difficult to commit crime with a small child in tow.

• Women are less likely to be involved in white-collar crime because the top jobs in industry and government are occupied by men.

• Many women do not have the technical knowledge to commit crimes like car theft.

• Adler (1975) argues that the more liberated women are in terms of job opportunities, the more likely they are to commit crime, e.g. white-collar crime.

- Box and Hale (1983) found no evidence that an increase in women's emancipation led to an increase in women's crime.
- Liberation is most likely to have affected the lives of middle-class women but most female crime is committed by lower-class women.

Reasons why women commit crime

- The feminisation of poverty and especially the increasing numbers of single-parent families headed by women may partly account for women who commit social security fraud or who fail to pay for their television licence.
- Walklate (1995) notes that the majority of female crimes are property crimes, e.g. shoplifting, which suggests that females rationally commit crime out of economic necessity, i.e. to provide children with food, toys, clothes etc.
- There is some evidence from research by Edwards (1981) that prostitution may be due to poverty caused by limited job opportunities coupled with women's low earning potential and low welfare benefits (i.e. inequalities generated by the patriarchal nature of society).
- Carlen's ethnographic study of women in prison (1988) concluded that some women made conscious and rational decisions to engage in crime — it was regarded as a positive response, as well as enjoyable and exciting, and a way of escaping from poverty.
- Croall suggests that for teenage girls, crimes may have little to do with poverty. They may be motivated by a drug habit (which often leads to prostitution and shoplifting), the search for excitement and the need to obtain designer clothes, which are seen by some of them as important in shaping their image and identity.
- Recently, moral panics have focused on violent girl gangs and alleged increases in female violence. Evidence from the USA (this is a severely under-researched area in the UK) suggests that girls from poverty-stricken backgrounds join street gangs because they feel a strong need to belong to a group and defend territory. However, such girls, despite their involvement in violence (this is not as intense as that experienced by males) and drug-pushing, still retain a strong sense of femininity, i.e. their primary role is to support male members of the gang as girlfriends etc.

Key concepts
police paternalism; chivalry factor; gender blindness; double deviants; sexualisation of delinquency; patriarchy; feminisation of poverty; ethnography; moral panics

Explanations for ethnic-minority crime

As we saw earlier, African-Caribbeans are over-represented in the official criminal statistics and in the prison population. The Asian crime rate, on the other hand, is lower than the overall crime rate.

- Morris (1994) argues that most crime is committed by the young, and ethnic-minority groups have a higher proportion of young people than the white population.

  Evaluation
  - If this were the case, young Asians would also be over-represented in the statistics as the young make up the majority of this group. However, this group does not feature heavily in the criminal statistics.

Policing and the courts

- Studies of policing (see pp. 19–22) indicate that police officers are more likely to stop, search and arrest young African-Caribbean males than any other group. Studies such as Holdaway (2000), and Lord McPherson's report (2000) into the death of Stephen Lawrence, illustrate the institutional racism of the police which produces an occupational culture in which negative stereotyping of African-Caribbeans, in particular, is the norm.
- Research by Hood (1989) indicates the possibility of some bias in the judicial process. He concluded that young African-Caribbean males were more likely to receive custodial sentences than young white males for the same type of offences.

  Evaluation
  - Left realists argue that while these biases may exist, the fact remains that in some inner-city areas of London, young African-Caribbean males do commit more crime than other social groups.

Blocked opportunities

- Cashmore (1989), drawing on the ideas of Merton, argues that young African-Caribbeans in Britain are encouraged like everybody else to pursue material success but their opportunities are blocked by factors such as racism, failing inner-city schools and unemployment. Young blacks experience anomie and alienation — they are aware that their situation arises from being black in a predominantly white society. They turn to street crime as a form of innovation and justify their criminal activities on the grounds that white society has given them nothing and they therefore have no obligation to follow white laws.

  Evaluation
  - Blocked opportunities are experienced by the majority of African-Caribbeans but Cashmore fails to explain why only a small proportion of young blacks actually turn to crime.

Marxist explanations

- Marxists such as Hall (1978) claim that black people have been criminalised by the British state because they represent a threat to authority and institutionalised racism (especially when they are involved in urban disorder, i.e. inner-city riots). Hall claims that a moral panic was constructed in the early 1970s around the street

crime of mugging, which effectively labelled the young African-Caribbean population as a criminal threat to the white population. This legitimated an aggressive
policing policy in black communities and also played the ideological role of
dividing the working class, i.e. setting white working-class people against black
working-class people. This distracted the working class from inequalities and
problems created by capitalism.

- Gilroy (1987), a radical criminologist, argues that crime committed by young
African-Caribbeans is political: it is frequently motivated by this group's interpretation of its position in British society. He argues that a lot of black street crime
is a deliberate expression of young black people's anger at the way white society
has historically treated black people (viz slavery and colonialism), and a conscious
reaction and resistance to the institutional racism of everyday life.

Evaluation

- The fact that most African-Caribbeans are law-abiding challenges the view that
crime is part of an anti-colonial or anti-racist struggle.
- The first generation of immigrants had first-hand experience of colonialism and
racism but did not turn to crime to make their protest.
- If African-Caribbean crime is a political protest against white racism, why are a great
number of victims of crime black?
- There is no empirical evidence of black youth having the political motives that
Gilroy identifies.

Left realism

- The left realists, Lea and Young, suggest that young blacks experience relative
deprivation in that they compare their economic position, especially access to
consumer goods, with their white peers. Their opportunities are likely to be blocked
because of institutional racism in employment, education, housing and day-to-
day dealings with the police. As a consequence they feel marginalised and
frustrated. Lea and Young suggest that some young blacks may respond to this
situation in a subcultural fashion, although they stress that crime is only one
subcultural response.

Evaluation

See evaluation points on left realism on p. 48.

Asian crime

- Asian crime may be low because Asians are less likely to be economically marginalised, i.e. they are more likely to be in employment or in business. Asian families
also exercise stricter controls over young people which may limit their opportunity for crime. Finally, Asian culture may provide a safety net if members 'fail' in
mainstream society, so Asian youth are less likely to be relatively deprived and
frustrated.

Evaluation

- There is evidence that Asian crime is rising.
- There have been concerns about the policing of violence against Asian communities.
- There have been accusations of police and judicial bias in the arrest and imprisonment of young Asians protesting about racism in their communities.

Key concepts

occupational culture; blocked opportunities; colonialism; crime as an anti-colonial struggle; institutional racism; relative deprivation; marginalisation; subcultures

Questions
&
Answers

This section of the guide provides you with six questions on the topic of **Crime and Deviance** in the style of the OCR examination. The first three questions are followed by a grade-C candidate response. These are on the right track but fail, for various reasons, to score very high marks.

Questions 1 to 4 also have a grade-A candidate response. It is important to note that these are not 'model' answers. These responses are not the only possible answers to these questions, nor are they necessarily the best. They represent one particular successful style, one that answers the question set and demonstrates the appropriate skills, especially using suitable concepts and studies, displaying a critical and evaluative awareness towards the material used and presenting a logically structured argument.

You must therefore not make the mistake of learning the A-grade responses parrot-fashion. Remember you have to be flexible and be able to respond to the specific demands of a question. It would be quite possible to take a different approach, or to use different material, or even to come to a different conclusion, and still gain very high marks.

Questions 5 and 6 are not accompanied by student answers. However, plans of action are included and you should use these to write your own responses. It is recommended that you spend some time revising the topics before answering the questions, which you should answer under timed conditions with no notes.

Examiner's comments

The candidate answers are accompanied by examiner's comments. These are preceded by the icon *e* and indicate where credit is due. For the grade-A answers, the examiner shows you what it is that enables the candidate to score so highly. Particular attention is given to the candidate's use of the examinable skills: knowledge and understanding; interpretation and analysis; and evaluation. For the grade-C answers, the examiner points out areas for improvement, specific problems and common errors. You are also invited to rewrite the answer in order to gain higher marks, and some pointers are given to show you how you might do this.

The role of the mass media in defining crime and deviance

Outline and assess the view that the mass media have a disproportionate influence over societal reactions to crime and deviance.

■ ■ ■

Answer to question 1: grade-C candidate

There are those who believe that the mass media have too much influence over the policing of certain crimes. For example, recently we have seen newspapers and television spend a lot of time reporting about paedophilia, and this has put a lot of pressure on the police and government to do something about it — although this is a good thing.

e This candidate would have got off to a better start by writing an introduction. This would set the scene for the debate by identifying the 'view' contained in the title as one held by interactionists who subscribe to moral-panic theory. The introduction could also briefly explain some of the terms of the question, e.g. the meaning of 'societal reactions to crime and deviance'. Another weakness of this candidate's opening paragraph is that the final statement, 'this is a good thing', is assertion, which should always be avoided.

The first sociologist who did any work on the relationship between the media and crime was Jock Young. He studied hippy drug-takers in the 1960s and the media reaction to them. He points out that the general public knew very little about the hippy habit of smoking dope until the tabloid newspapers started running stories about it. In fact, Young argues that the newspapers got most of their information about hippies and drugs from police officers who did not like the lazy lifestyle of the hippies. Journalists were happy to go along with the police because stories about drugs were newsworthy. They became even more so when celebrities like members of the Rolling Stones were arrested.

e This section provides a reasonably good description of Young's work, although it is a little generalised in style and lacks any reference to concepts.

Young argues that newspaper attention led to a social reaction from the general public, with other newspapers and politicians calling for something to be done about the 'problem' of the hippies. This is called a moral panic. Hippies were made out to be folk devils, i.e. a threat to society.

e A more precise definition of 'moral panic' would gain more marks. The concept of 'folk devils' is dealt with slightly more satisfactorily.

This had two main effects. First, the hippies became more secretive about their activities — an underground culture developed amongst them and dope-smoking came to be seen as a symbol of rebellion. This attracted more young people to the activity. Second, the police reacted in a more negative way. They raided hippy houses and actually set up drug squads to target the problem. Young argues then that the moral panic led to a worsening of the problem because dope became more difficult to obtain and criminal gangs moved in to supply it and introduced other harder drugs. Young therefore concludes that the mass media had a very influential role to play in how society and the forces of law and order reacted to dope-smoking.

e This section is fairly accurate as a sociological summary of Young's work, especially with regard to the consequences of the moral panic. The candidate shows some interpretation and analysis skills by focusing on societal reaction in the form of policing and young people's reaction to the moral panic.

Young and Cohen refer to the media as moral entrepreneurs, meaning that journalists and editors focus on particular stories because they believe them to be newsworthy, i.e. they will sell newspapers and attract a television audience. However, the moral entrepreneurs are also concerned about society. They know what worries their audiences in terms of crime and morality. The media therefore claim that society is in moral decline, usually because of the activities of a younger generation which is seen as undermining tradition, authority and decency.

e This is a valid interpretation of Cohen and Young's explanation for why moral panics emerge. The use of concepts such as 'moral entrepreneurs', 'newsworthy' and 'morality' would be rewarded.

These ideas fit in very nicely with labelling theory which says there is no such thing as deviance. People like Becker argue that deviance is a matter of interpretation, i.e. it needs someone to recognise or to define a particular action as wrong. Interactionists argue that we live in a society which has lots of different groups with different values living in it. Who is to say what or who is deviant? However, interactionists argue that the powerful are able to define what is 'right' or 'wrong' behaviour. The 'powerful' seem to be made up of a number of different groups, e.g. men probably make rules for women, the older generation makes rules for the young while the middle class makes rules for the working class. Cohen argues that people like the police and the media operate on behalf of the powerful to label the activities of particular groups as deviant. Moral panics therefore occur as part of a labelling process which aims to manipulate public opinion on behalf of those groups which have power. Media concerns about the morals of the younger generation seen in moral panics about drugs, underage sex, punks, ecstasy and dance music are really the societal reactions of the powerful older generation which makes up the establishment.

e A good knowledge and understanding of interactionist theory is demonstrated and moral-panic theory is reasonably well linked to labelling. Interpretation and analysis skills are shown too in the links between moral panics, labelling and social reaction.

Moral-panic theory has been criticised. Marxists argue that moral-panic theory and labelling theory are actually very vague as to why moral panics come about and who has the power to cause them. It is not clear who benefits from them.

e This is a good evaluative point but it lacks development. There should be some exploration from a Marxist perspective as to who benefits from moral panics.

Moral-panic theory has been very useful to our sociological understanding of the influence the media have over public opinion, the police and the government. However, left realists argue that moral-panic theory exaggerates the influence of the media over such social reaction to crime. They argue that victim surveys in the inner cities show clearly that social reaction is shaped by the reality of crime in these areas — most people have been attacked, robbed or burgled, or know someone who has, usually by young people for drug-related motives. It is this experience that makes people react in the way they do to crime rather than what they read in newspapers or see on their televisions.

e This is a very good evaluative paragraph. It highlights a strength of moral-panic theory and accurately criticises the theory from a left-realist perspective.

e Overall, this candidate demonstrates a reasonably good knowledge and understanding of the relationship between the mass media and crime. The chosen studies are summarised clearly, although the candidate is not always focused on how the media shape societal reactions. The candidate would therefore score 17/28 for knowledge and understanding. The material selected is generally relevant, if a little dated. Most of the analysis is appropriate, but the question of societal reaction needs to be addressed more consistently. Consequently, the candidate would score 11/16 for interpretation and analysis. Evaluation, however, only appears in the last two paragraphs and requires a little more development. For example, crucial criticisms made by left realists are omitted. 10/16 marks would be awarded for evaluation.

Overall mark: 38/60

Task

(a) Think about how you would reorganise the section describing moral panics into distinct stages, documenting how the media shape the nature of both the panic and the societal reaction.

(b) Write 400 words evaluating moral-panic theory in general and specific studies of moral panics.

■ ■ ■

Answer to question 1: grade-A candidate

There are essentially three ways in which the mass media can be seen to have a disproportionate influence over societal reactions to crime. First, critics of the official criminal statistics suggest that crime rates are artificially amplified by the mass media's construction of moral panics which increase fear of crime and the general public's reporting of particular offences. Moreover, the authorities are put under tremendous pressure to deal with the problem highlighted by the panic and, consequently, may react with heavier policing and stiffer sentencing which further increase the statistics. Second, interactionist sociologists argue that the mass media are therefore one of the key agents involved in the social construction of crime, i.e. it is argued that the media as an agency may socially react to and define deviance on behalf of powerful groups in society. Finally, Marxists see mass media agencies as part of an ideological state apparatus manipulating societal reaction to particular types of crime in order to divide and rule the working classes and divert attention away from crises of capitalism.

> ℮ This introduction clearly sets the scene for the debate about moral panics. Three inter-related sociological approaches to moral panics are outlined and the role of social reaction is highlighted in each.

There is a view that the official criminal statistics are both unreliably gathered and invalid in the picture of crime that they paint. It is argued that such statistics tell us more about the various people involved in their collection — i.e. victims, the general public who report crime, the police, the courts and, of course, the media — than they tell us about crimes and criminals. The focus of much sociology has been on the ability of tabloid newspapers in particular to orchestrate moral panics and, consequently, public or societal reactions to particular events. Cohen notes that societies appear to be subject every now and then to periods of moral panic. What he means by this is that a particular activity or person or social group comes to be defined as a threat to social values, and therefore order, because of the nature and style of media reporting.

> ℮ This paragraph demonstrates excellent knowledge and understanding of the relationship between moral panics and the social construction of criminal statistics. Interpretation and analysis skills are also shown in the clear focus on the concept of societal reaction. There is also an accurate definition of 'moral panic'.

Both Cohen and Young noted that moral panics are organised in stages. First, the media take an interest in a particular activity and deem it newsworthy, i.e. interesting enough to sell newspapers. The style of the reporting is usually sensationalised in terms of the tone of the language and headlines used. This 'hysterical' style usually exaggerates the threat posed by the group or activity but is enough to generate a negative societal reaction in the form of public fear and demands that something be done. Ben-Yehuda calls this first stage 'concern' and notes that it usually results in a consensus that is convincing in its view that society is threatened.

Second, in follow-up articles, journalists demonise, i.e. negatively label, members of the so-called deviant group by allocating symbolic features to them, e.g. styles of dress, behaviour etc., so that the general public can recognise, avoid and possibly report them. The deviant group is therefore exposed to sustained media and public hostility and turned into 'folk devils', i.e. the enemy of society. Third, Ben-Yehuda notes that the consensus is reinforced by the emergence of powerful moral entrepreneurs, e.g. politicians who both simplify the causes of the deviancy, i.e. moral decline, disrespect for the older generation etc., and insist on 'stamping down hard' on the so-called problem group. This moralist intervention leads to a disproportionate attempt to control the problem group. The police stop, search and arrest members of the group more frequently, magistrates and judges pass heavier sentences and governments introduce new laws banning the problem behaviour. The societal reaction, in terms of authority, is therefore excessive. In addition, the general public reacts to the publicity by reporting more crime. Finally, Ben-Yehuda points out that moral panics have high volatility — they come in short bursts and often do not last more than a couple of weeks, mainly because journalists lose interest in them because of their declining newsworthiness. However, in terms of the official criminal statistics, the damage is done because the societal reaction, i.e. in the form of more reporting of crime and police attention, has resulted in a rise in the crime rate which ironically convinces the general public that the problem was very real in the first place.

🖉 This is a substantive and focused section which demonstrates excellent knowledge and understanding of the theory of moral panics. It uses concepts liberally and accurately and name-checks a modern moral panic theorist, i.e. Ben-Yehuda, rather than over-relying on Cohen and Young. It also demonstrates interpretation and analysis skills by returning to the concept of societal reaction in the final sentence.

Young's study of drug-takers in the 1960s argued that moral panics lead to further deviance because they often result in the setting up of oppositional underground subcultures which actively encourage drug-taking as a symbol of resistance. Other sociologists, such as Thornton and Redhead, note that a moral panic arose in the early 1990s over dance music and especially ecstasy use among teenagers. This had the effect of attracting young people to the oppositional e-generation subculture which had evolved out of the moral panic. Membership of this was interpreted by young people as rejecting and challenging establishment definitions of normality and deviance.

🖉 Good knowledge and understanding of the effects of moral panics are demonstrated in this paragraph and confident use is made of concepts such as oppositional subcultures. A range of studies are also cited.

Left realists are critical of the implicit assumption within moral-panic theory that somehow crime is not 'real' but instead a media construction. On the basis of victim surveys conducted in inner-city areas, left realists point out that violent crime and property crime, such as burglary, are a serious problem in urban areas.

Levels of long-term drug addiction and the crime that results from this are a reality. Moreover, it is difficult, if not impossible, to measure empirically the effects of a moral panic upon social reaction and therefore upon the criminal statistics, or upon criminality and delinquency in general. Moral-panic theory often assumes such an effect but it is actually not proved. In addition, moral panics have focused on a range of anti-social behaviours, e.g. AIDS, welfare scroungers, mugging, football hooliganism and various deviant youth cultures, such as punks, but rarely on 'serious crime'. However, despite these criticisms, moral-panic theory has played an important role in our understanding of public perceptions of crime and police responses to it, and how these might be what Mooney et al. call 'social metaphors' for the social anxieties caused by major social change.

e This paragraph contains a good range of evaluation which is especially focused on societal reaction. Most importantly, the evaluation is positive as well as negative.

Interactionist sociologists are interested in moral panics because of their belief that deviance is a matter of social interpretation or reaction: powerful groups create the conditions for deviance by creating rules which less powerful groups are bound to break. Interactionists see the media (alongside the police) as agents of societal reaction working on behalf of the powerful to label, stereotype and control the behaviour of less powerful groups. In fact, interactionists, like Lemert, actually argue that the societal reaction rather than the labelled activity is the real problem of law and order, because such labels can have profound negative consequences for those who have been labelled, i.e. they may react by increasing their levels of deviance because they have been ostracised by family, friends and employers.

e This is an excellent theoretical link which demonstrates perceptive knowledge and understanding of the theory as well as focusing on the central element of the question, i.e. societal reaction.

Interactionist theories of moral panic have been criticised by left realists for romanticising crime in that they portray deviants as victims. Left realists argue that this ignores the very real damage and fear caused by crime. Marxists are also critical because they believe interactionists are too vague about the origins of power and who benefits from moral panics. They argue that moral panics are not surprising considering that the media functions on behalf of the capitalist class to transmit ruling-class ideology and divide and rule the working class.

e Sustained evaluation is constructed here from two theoretical positions in a confident and accurate fashion.

Hall argues that moral panics usually occur when capitalism is undergoing crisis and the working class begins to actively question the management of capitalism. He argues that a moral panic was generated in the early 1970s around the crime of 'mugging' which was labelled by the media as a crime mainly committed by young blacks against white people. This allegedly had the ideological effect of manipulating the societal reaction of the white working class so that it turned against the black working class. Hall argues that this moral panic defused the working-class threat to the bourgeoisie's domination of the capitalist state and allowed the ruling class to politically censure and control the working class under the guise of controlling crime. However, Marxist moral-panic theory is almost impossible to confirm because it is unlikely that sociologists can uncover evidence that such panics are deliberately manufactured. As left realists argue, to dismiss the crime highlighted by moral panics as ruling-class mystification is to ignore the human suffering caused by such crime.

e The candidate demonstrates a perceptive understanding of Marxist theory which is focused on the question of social reaction. The criticism of Marxism is convincing.

Overall, both interactionist and Marxist sociologists suggest that the mass media has a disproportionate influence over social reactions to crime and deviance. There is evidence that media reporting can shape the reaction of the general public and particularly the police towards certain groups and activities. Interactionists and Marxists disagree as to the reasons for such influence. However, left realists are sceptical of these claims and argue that societal reactions to crime are caused by direct experience of crime rather than media reporting.

e This summative conclusion addresses the theoretical fundamentals of the question and reinforces the fact that this candidate has focused on the question consistently throughout.

e Overall, this essay demonstrates a wide-ranging and detailed knowledge and understanding of theories, evidence and concepts relating to the relationship between the media and societal reactions to crime and deviance. There is a clear understanding of what is meant by societal reactions, moral panics and other key ideas. The candidate would therefore score 28/28 for knowledge and understanding. The material selected is both highly relevant and contemporary. Both theory and evidence are organised in a way that is always focused on the question set. The candidate would be awarded 16/16 for interpretation and analysis. Evaluation is well developed throughout, aimed at all theories discussed, and balanced in its assessment of both strengths and weaknesses. The candidate would therefore score **16/16** for evaluation. It is difficult to see how this candidate could have improved this response.

Overall mark: 60/60

Structuralist theories of crime

Outline and assess the view that the organisation of capitalism is responsible for the crime committed by those at the bottom of the socioeconomic order.

■ ■ ■

Answer to question 2: grade-C candidate

If we look at who is at the bottom of the socioeconomic order, we can see that there are three major groups, i.e. the white working class, the black working class and the poor, especially the long-term unemployed and those who have never worked. The criminal statistics seem to suggest that these groups are more likely to be arrested and convicted, but we cannot trust these figures.

e The candidate rightly identifies the groups at the bottom of the socioeconomic order. Unfortunately, he or she does not address what is meant by 'the organisation of capitalism'. The evaluative reference to the criminal statistics is too vague.

These poorest groups commit crimes for a variety of reasons. Some sociologists say it is because they subscribe to deviant or criminal values. For example, Cohen did some work on working-class delinquent gangs in the USA and found that they were not interested in educational qualifications. In fact, they felt frustrated because schools did not give them status and society did not give them good jobs, so they formed delinquent subcultures which gave status to each other on the basis of anti-social behaviour. The more 'bad' their behaviour, the more status they got.

e The material on Cohen is broadly correct but it is not clear how it relates to the question. It does not address capitalism or how such crime might be related to being poor or unemployed.

Not everybody agrees with this view. David Matza says that we are all potentially deviant or criminal because we all subscribe to subterranean values, i.e. the need for excitement etc., but most of us live these out in legal ways, e.g. sport. Others, such as working-class males, do it on a Saturday night whilst on a pub run and are likely to come into contact with the police.

e This paragraph is peripheral to the question set. Its tone is also very assertive and opinionated.

Marxists blame capitalism for working-class crime. David Gordon argues that we are socialised into capitalist ideas like materialism and consumerism which makes us greedy. A lot of people also feel resentful and jealous because of capitalism. These are the people at the bottom of society who look at the living standards everybody else has got and feel envious. So capitalism puts 'criminal ideas' into people's heads.

e The candidate focuses on the central issue of capitalism reasonably well, although again the style is assertive rather than sociological.

This is not dissimilar to what Robert Merton argues. He is a functionalist thinker who blames crime on society rather than the individual. He argues that capitalist society puts its members under a lot of pressure because it strongly encourages them to pursue the cultural goal of material success. Everywhere we look we are bombarded with advertising messages saying 'buy this' and 'buy that', 'get interest-free credit', 'keep up with the Joneses' etc. We are also convinced by society that all these things are within our grasp — all we have to do is work hard at school, get qualifications, get a decent job, work hard, get promoted etc. However, society cannot provide us all with good qualifications or well-paid jobs. Most of us fail at school or become unemployed — often through no fault of our own. Merton recognises that people at the bottom of society are more likely to miss out than most because schools benefit middle-class children more than working-class children, and because economic recession and unemployment hit the children of the poor more than the children of the rich.

e The candidate rightly sees the connection between Merton and Marxism. The material on Merton is good and focuses well on capitalism, although the assertion that 'most of us fail at school' is exaggerated.

Merton said that people in capitalist societies who experienced this problem are more likely to feel frustrated or angry because they couldn't achieve the material success they were promised. Most did not turn to crime but instead conformed by working hard or by trying to get a job. However, some people 'innovated' — this means that they turned to illegal means to get rich or become better off. Others dropped out of the system altogether whilst others were so angry at the way the capitalist system worked that they sought to replace it with a new system altogether through violent, revolutionary means.

e This is a reasonable summary of what Merton says about how people adapt to blocked opportunities in the capitalist system. The response continues to focus on the question set.

Merton is therefore blaming the organisation of capitalist society and saying that it is understandable that people at the bottom of society commit crime. He has been criticised mainly by Marxists like Laurie Taylor, who said that his view of society can be likened to a fruit machine (most people carry on playing hoping for the jackpot, the innovators stick foreign coins in it etc.), but that he does not say who put the machine there in the first place and who empties it. What Taylor means is that capitalist society benefits the rich, who make the laws and also benefit from white-collar and corporate crime.

e The candidate directly addresses the question and demonstrates good interpretation and analysis skills. The evaluation too is both focused and relevant.

Other Marxists blame capitalist societies in other ways. The new criminologists, Taylor, Walton and Young, argue that the working classes are unhappy with their position in capitalist society and commit crime as a form of political protest. They argue that crime is a revolutionary activity — criminals are like Robin Hood stealing from the rich to redistribute wealth to the poor. However, this is a bit romanticised. Left realists point out that the rich can afford to protect themselves from crime and, as a result, the main victims of working-class crime are usually other working-class people. Gilroy does not blame capitalism for black crime. He blames slavery, colonialism and institutional racism. He argues that black youths feel resentful about these things and commit crime against white society because of this. However, a lot of victims of black crime are black themselves.

> *e* There is a lot going on in this paragraph. The candidate refers to three perspectives on crime but doesn't really get to grips with any of them. Consequently, all three summaries are a little vague, although two (i.e. the new criminology and Gilroy) demonstrate interpretation and analysis in their focus on capitalism. There is also some evaluation in this paragraph, but the points made deserve more attention.

Finally, right realists say that people commit crime because they can see that it benefits them. In other words, punishments are light if you are caught. They argue that we have got to increase the costs of crime by making sure that punishments are tougher. They believe in 'zero tolerance' and 'three strikes and you're out', i.e. people should be sent to prison for minor crimes. Left realists argue that this is unfair and we should try and understand the criminal mentality: people commit crime because of the organisation of society. For example, black people are more likely to be economically deprived compared with similar social groups because of institutional racism. They lack any power to change their situation and therefore it is not surprising that they turn to crime. We therefore need to look for ways to improve the economic situation of these groups and to give them more power to legally change their situation.

> *e* The candidate loses his or her way in this paragraph and the material presented here is at a tangent to the question set. The material on left realism in particular is a wasted opportunity: with one extra sentence this could easily have been related to capitalism. It is unclear how the right-realist material relates to the question.

> *e* Overall, this candidate demonstrates more than basic knowledge and understanding of functionalist and Marxist theories but doesn't really get to grips in any detail with the central principles of these two theories with regard to capitalism. There is conceptual knowledge but this is underdeveloped — the candidate misses opportunities to develop ideas such as institutional racism, relative deprivation etc. Consequently, the candidate would score only **17/28** for knowledge and understanding. In terms of interpretation and analysis, the candidate takes a while to address the specifics of the question, although once this has been done it is reasonably well sustained throughout the discussion of Merton and Marxist

approaches. However, focus is lost in the final section and it is not clear how right-realist or left-realist approaches relate to capitalism. The candidate would therefore score 11/12 for interpretation and analysis. Evaluation too takes some time to develop and although there are some reasonably clear references to weaknesses in the latter half, these deserve further development, and strengths are generally ignored. The candidate would therefore be awarded 10/16 for evaluation.

Overall mark: 38/60

Task

Think how you might insert key sentences into this essay to improve the scores both for interpretation and analysis and for evaluation. Remember that interpretation and analysis are essentially about addressing the question while evaluation should focus on both the strengths and weaknesses of theories, evidence and concepts.

■ ■ ■

Answer to question 2: grade-A candidate

The view in the essay title is a structuralist one, i.e. these sociologists, who can be functionalist or Marxist, argue that people's behaviour is shaped, determined and constrained by the social organisation of societies, i.e. their social structure. Powerful social forces, such as value consensus, social class, patriarchy etc., are seen to be produced by the organisation of society and cultures and consequently push people in the direction of potentially criminal and deviant behaviour. This view of social behaviour is rejected by both interpretivist and realist sociologists who argue that social actors have the ability to make choices and decisions about their actions, i.e. they can resist social influences or negotiate their way through them. In the final analysis, criminal behaviour is the result of people interpreting their place in society and reacting accordingly.

e This is an excellent introduction. The candidate clearly contextualises the view in the question in terms of a theoretical debate between structuralist and interpretivist sociologists. There is confident and knowledgeable use of concepts.

One of the first sociologists to focus on the idea that society might be responsible for the criminality of the poor and working class, i.e. those at the bottom of the socioeconomic order, was the functionalist sociologist Robert Merton. Merton argues that a great deal of criminality arises out of value consensus in that capitalist society sets all its members cultural goals, the most dominant of which is material success or wealth acquisition. Such goals are constantly encouraged via a culture of consumerism, media advertising and the fact that material success is rewarded with high status. However, Merton points out that society fails to provide all its members with the institutional means of achieving these goals. We are constantly encouraged to acquire educational qualifications and to work for financial rewards in the long term but through no fault of their own, social groups at the bottom of society are denied access to these legitimate means. Their

opportunities are blocked by the strain between the goals and the means and this results in anomie, i.e. feelings of an inability to fit in, confusion and alienation.

e Those at the bottom of the socioeconomic order are quickly defined. This paragraph demonstrates an excellent understanding and articulation of Merton's ideas and focuses on capitalist society. It is analytical and conceptually very confident in terms of the range of concepts used.

Most members of lower socioeconomic groups cope with such anomie by continuing to conform to value consensus and the law. However, a significant minority react to strain by abandoning the legitimate means. These people innovate by turning to crime to achieve the cultural goal of financial success. Others, however, reject both the goals and means. Retreatists drop out of society, perhaps by turning to drugs or alcohol or even suicide. Others reject both the goals and means and replace them with an alternative set, e.g. communism. Merton, then, argues that crime arises naturally out of the cultural goals society's members are socialised into by the educational system, families and mass media. Criminals are not that different to the rest of society — they are motivated by the same goals and only turn to criminal action after being let down by social institutions like education.

e Excellent knowledge and understanding are demonstrated in this paragraph. The interpretation and analysis are focused on capitalism.

Merton's theory has been influential and the concept of anomie has been used in a range of sociological explanations that link crime to economic disadvantage, e.g. left realism. Sumner claims that Merton is right to focus on the disillusion created by capitalism and this aspect has certainly struck a chord with Marxist sociologists. However, Merton's theory does have problems: it is essentially a theory which focuses on economic crime and consequently it doesn't really explain violent crime or juvenile delinquency (which does not normally involve economic gain). It also assumes that the whole of society shares the same material goals, but surveys indicate that the poor may not do this because they realistically do not believe that they can achieve material success. It is also not clear why people choose the paths they do, i.e. why do most people conform rather than innovate? Merton's theory is criticised too for being overdeterministic, i.e. it strongly implies that most people passively accept their lot. However, this may be a little unfair on Merton in that he does suggest some groups do innovate, retreat, rebel etc. Marxists criticise Merton because they feel that he does not deal with the concept of power adequately. He fails to ask who benefits from the capitalist system and especially the laws that underpin it. In particular, he fails to recognise that the rich and the powerful commit crime and that this is obviously not the result of blocked opportunities and anomie.

e This evaluation paragraph includes convincing positive and negative assessment from a range of theoretical positions.

Marxists, therefore, have constructed an alternative structuralist theory of crime based on the social organisation of capitalism. They argue that crime is an inevitable by-product of capitalism and the class inequality that this economic system generates. In their view, capitalism is characterised by class inequality and is therefore grossly unfair in its distribution of wealth, income and power. Those at the bottom of the socioeconomic order are likely to face poverty, unemployment, homelessness etc. and crimes committed by the poor and disadvantaged are a realistic response to these aspects of class inequality.

e Interpretation and analysis are well focused on addressing the fundamentals of the question such as capitalism and those at the bottom of the socioeconomic hierarchy.

Moreover, Gordon argues that crime is encouraged by the dominant ideology of capitalism which values competition, individualism, materialism etc. Greed is generally regarded as good in capitalist societies. The hierarchical nature of capitalism may also encourage crime motivated by envy and alienation and powerlessness — especially crimes of violence which may result from feelings of hostility and the need to compensate for lack of economic power. Marxists are surprised how conformist the working classes actually are and argue that crime rates are low considering the organisation of capitalism. However, Althusser argues that the reason for this is the ideological apparatus of the law which functions to protect the interests of the capitalist class (i.e. wealth, private property and profit) and to give the working class and poor the impression that all members of society are equal in the eyes of the law (i.e. by passing weak and ineffective laws such as health and safety legislation). However, Althusser also notes that the ruling class has the power to prevent laws being passed which are not in its interests. Law enforcement is selective too and, consequently, white-collar and corporate crime, which are committed by the rich and powerful, are rarely prosecuted.

e Excellent knowledge and understanding of Marxism are demonstrated here.

A neo-Marxist approach — the new criminology — is critical of the determinism of traditional Marxism because the poor and the working class tend to be portrayed as passive victims of capitalism who are driven to crime by social influences, e.g. class inequality, which are beyond their control. Taylor, Walton and Young, however, reject this view and insist that crime is a product of the way the working class and ethnic-minority groups interpret their structural position at the bottom of the socioeconomic hierarchy. Crime, from this neo-Marxist perspective, is deliberate and, most importantly, political because it arises out of a conscious frustration with injustice, exploitation and alienation. Crimes such as burglary and theft aim to redistribute wealth and income whilst vandalism is a symbolic attack on society's obsession with property. Criminals, then, are not the passive victims of capitalism — they are actively struggling to change capitalism for the better. The

question

ruling class, in reaction to this threat, uses the law and repressive bodies such as the police as well as media moral panics to criminalise the working class in order to control this threat to the maintenance of capitalism.

e This paragraph displays perceptive knowledge and understanding, and consistently and confidently addresses the question set.

This Marxist theory of crime has attracted heavy criticism from realist approaches. Right realism argues that crime is the product of conscious decision-making, i.e. criminals rationally weigh up the costs of crime compared with its benefits. Hirschi notes that for certain groups at the bottom of the socioeconomic hierarchy, i.e. the welfare-dependent underclass, the benefits of crime often outweigh the costs in terms of the risks of being caught and the degree of punishment. Right realism rejects the view that crime is political. Instead, crime involves a rational decision to act deviantly because it benefits the individual. Right realists recommend that punishments be increased as a realistic deterrence to crime and that saturation policing, i.e. 'zero tolerance', be introduced to increase the risks of being caught.

e Here the candidate demonstrates sustained and convincing criticism of the Marxist view from a right-realist perspective.

Left realists, on the other hand, reject the Marxist view of crime as over-romantic. They argue that the organisation of capitalism does produce economic and social problems for the working class and the poor, especially those of African-Caribbean origin. These groups are more likely to experience 'relative deprivation', i.e. they interpret their economic situation as deprived compared with other social groups such as their middle-class peers. They also experience feelings of marginalisation, i.e. they feel that there is little they can do to change their situation. They may even feel that they are being persecuted by groups such as the police. Some members of these groups turn to criminal subcultures to solve this situation, although the majority conform and abide by the law.

e Excellent knowledge and understanding and interpretation and analysis skills are demonstrated in this paragraph.

Left realism therefore rejects the idea that crime is political and anti-capitalist. Rather, left realists point out that most victims of black and working-class crime are black and working class themselves. However, left realism fails to provide empirical evidence that young criminals are experiencing relative deprivation and powerlessness and that crime is a response to their interpretations of these factors. In fact, both structuralist and interpretivist theories of crime suffer from a similar inability to provide empirical evidence of how criminals themselves interpret their criminality.

e This is an evaluative conclusion which intelligently suggests that all these theories are flawed because of the lack of empirical evidence on how working-class criminals interpret their criminal actions.

e Overall, this essay demonstrates a wide-ranging and detailed knowledge and under-standing of structuralist theories, concepts and evidence relating to them. The candidate shows a perceptive and articulate ability to address the debate consis-tently throughout and sees the need to make frequent connections between capitalism, crime and the lower socioeconomic order. Evaluation is sustained throughout in detail and focuses intelligently and substantively on both strengths and weaknesses of a range of theories. This candidate would score full marks across all three skills.

Overall mark: 60/60

Measuring crime

Outline and assess the view that the official criminal statistics tell us more about the people involved in their collection than they tell us about crime and criminals.

■ ■ ■

Answer to question 3: grade-C candidate

The official criminal statistics tell us a great deal about crime, although not all sociologists would agree with this observation. However, if we examine them, we can see that since the 1970s, most types of crime have been on the increase and that, although there was a fall in the amount of crime in the 1990s, the crime rate has risen again in recent years. Most crime is property crime, although violent crime has risen slowly so that it now makes up 15% of all crime. We can also get some ideas about what criminals are like by looking at the statistics. They tell us that criminals are often under 21 years old, and evidence from the occupational backgrounds of convicted criminals suggests that 80% are in manual jobs, i.e. from the working class. We can also see that black people are disproportionately found in prison. We can therefore conclude from these statistics that criminals are generally working class and black.

e This essay begins well with a generally accurate review of trends in crime and what the statistics tell us about the social characteristics of criminality.

The Home Office, which collects the statistics from the police and the courts, sees nothing wrong with them. The statistics have been collected scientifically so they are regarded as reliable. They are based on reports to the police by the general public and crimes recorded by the police, who are very trustworthy. They are also valid — that is, they give a true and realistic picture of crime according to politicians who base their law and order policies on them.

e So far, so good — the candidate rightly focuses on how official agencies view the statistics.

Not all sociologists agree with the statistics. They point out that crime is like an iceberg. Not all of it can be seen — a lot of it is under the surface. The bit above the surface is the crime that has been reported and recorded but there is a dark figure of unreported and unrecorded crime.

e A pertinent evaluative point is made, though the iceberg analogy is a little long-winded.

Sometimes the law changes or police forces change their counting rules and this complicates our ideas about the amount of crime out there. For example, recently the police had to add new crimes to their list, e.g. racist attacks. This makes it very difficult to say whether crimes are increasing or decreasing. A further compli-cation is that the police themselves might 'forget' to record crime. Clear-up rates for some crimes are very poor, especially for burglary, so some police forces might be tempted not to record burglaries because they might look bad. What is worrying is that sociologists have worked out that for every 100 crimes committed, only 27 are recorded by the police and only five cleared up in the form of a caution or conviction.

e This section includes some very relevant evaluation of the statistics, but there is a danger that the essay is turning into generalised commentary. Little evidence has been offered so far. There is also no theoretical context.

Sociologists like Andy Pilkington argue that when crime goes up, this is not a real increase — just that more people are reporting crime that has always existed. For example, more women are coming forward and reporting rape because they feel that the police will now treat them sympathetically (compared with in the past). In addition, people are growing more intolerant of property crime because they are becoming obsessed with materialism and consumerism. More insurance too will encourage people to report crime.

e The Pilkington reference is broadly valid, as is the reference to insurance. However, it is not clear how materialism/consumerism impacts on the criminal statistics.

Other sociologists like Holdaway blame the police for crime. Interactionist sociol-ogists argue that the statistics do not tell the whole truth about crime because police officers stop some social groups more than others. It is said that if you are a young black person living in London, you are more likely than a young white person to be stopped and arrested. This may cause hostility in young black people who might end up being more aggressive towards the police. Evidence from feminist sociologists indicates that young men are more likely to be stopped than young women (although the women are more likely to be cautioned than the men). So, the statistics may actually tell us more about police practices that they tell us about black or male criminal behaviour. Hood argues that similar practices can be seen in the courtroom. Judges are biased against working-class offenders and they do not like to prosecute white-collar crime.

e The material here is reasonably accurate but very superficial for an A2 essay. Holdaway's work deserves more substantial discussion, and material on race should be pursued in greater depth, with references made to contemporary studies such as the McPherson Report. The reference to Hood and judges tells us very little.

So, are the statistics correct? Self-report surveys tell us that most people have committed crime at some stage in their lives (usually when they are young), but most are not caught. In addition, the British Crime Survey tells us that a lot of victims do not report crimes because they do not have a lot of faith in the police. So these methods suggest that perhaps criminal statistics are not entirely reliable.

e This section accurately uses the concept of reliability to question the statistics and demonstrates reasonably good knowledge and understanding of self-reports and the British Crime Survey.

Finally, Marxists argue that the criminal statistics only tell us what the ruling class wants us to hear, i.e. that the 'real' criminals are those at the bottom of society — the working class and black people. Marxists conclude that we cannot trust these statistics because they ignore crimes committed by the powerful themselves. They exist only to fool us. Not everybody agrees with this. Left realists like Young and Lea and right realists like Murray argue that the statistics are correct in their picture of the working-class and black criminal. Murray, for example, believes criminality is the product of a deviant underclass. Young and Lea, on the other hand, argue that young working-class and black people do commit more crime than other social groups because they are poor and powerless.

e This final paragraph contains some relevant evaluation of the statistics, although all three perspectives are underdeveloped for an essay at this level. The candidate is often vague and doesn't always address the issues, e.g. it is not clear why the statistics exist to fool us or what a deviant underclass is or what is meant by 'poor and powerless'. All these points require further exploration. This superficial knowledge undermines the strength of the arguments raised.

e Overall, this candidate demonstrates some reasonable knowledge in terms of the debate about criminal statistics but fails to stamp any theoretical understanding upon the essay structure. Concepts are used reasonably well but evidence, in terms of studies, is underutilised. The candidate would therefore only receive 16/28 marks for knowledge and understanding. There is some attempt to address the question, but it is not very consistent and does not explain very well the social construction of the statistics in terms of what they tell us about groups like the police, victims etc. Therefore, the candidate would only be awarded 10/16 for interpretation and analysis. Evaluation is disappointing and is mainly implicit in a juxtaposition of views, although the last paragraph lifts it slightly. The candidate would score 9/16 for this skill.

Overall mark: 35/60

Task

Write four 100-word explainations of how the behaviour of each of the following groups may artificially inflate or deflate the criminal statistics: victims, the mass media, the police and the capitalist class.

■ ■ ■

Answer to question 3: grade-A candidate

This view is held by interpretivist and Marxist critics of the official criminal statistics (OCS), who argue that such statistics are a social construction rather than an objective, scientific and reliable measurement of crime. Moreover, interpretivists argue that the statistics tell us more about victims, the general public, the media, the police and the courts than they tell us about criminality. Marxists take this critique one step further by arguing that the statistics tell us more about the priorities of the capitalist class. However, not all agree with these critiques. Left realists have recently concluded that the official statistics do reflect the reality of crime.

e Note how this candidate sets the scene for the debate and locates the arguments about the reliability and validity of the statistics in the context of three theoretical approaches.

The OCS are collected quarterly by the Home Office and have generally demonstrated an increase in the volume of crime since the 1970s. Both property crime, which makes up 85% of crime, and violent crime (15%) rose dramatically until the mid-1990s, although property crime has since fallen while violent crime has tended to rise slowly. Governments have been very keen on the OCS and used them to determine their law and order policies. For example, in the 1980s juvenile crime rates increased and the Conservative government of the period introduced the 'short sharp shock' in the form of military-style detention centres. Most recently, concern about crime has prompted government interest in zero tolerance, punishing parents for their children's crimes and passing laws to prevent anti-social behaviour.

e Excellent knowledge and understanding of crime trends and how these relate to social policy issues are demonstrated here.

Interpretivist sociologists, however, are sceptical about the value of the OCS. It is suggested that they tell us more about the priorities and experiences of particular social groups than they tell us about crime and criminality. Pilkington notes that the OCS do not account for all the crime committed in the UK — only for those crimes which are recognised as such by victims and crimes detected by the police. The British Crime Survey shows that up to 75% of crime known to victims may not be reported because victims lack confidence in the ability of the police to catch offenders or they think the offence is too 'trivial' to report.

e Note the interpretation and analysis skills reflected in the reference to the essay title and the accurate links to Pilkington and the British Crime Survey to support the case that statistics tell us more about the attitudes of victims than about levels of crime.

In what seems a contradictory trend, we can see that some victims may be more willing now than in the past to report particular types of crime. It is likely that statistics for some property crimes have risen because as society has grown more affluent, property-orientated people have become less tolerant of burglary and more willing to report it. Insurance too is more widespread, and a police report is required to back up any claim. Social changes too, especially the improvement in women's opportunities, may mean that women are more willing to report rape and domestic violence (although these crimes are still under-reported). Overall,

then, we can see that the statistics may reflect important changes in the attitudes of victims which make them either willing or unwilling to come forward and report crime.

ℓ The candidate recognises that the collection of statistics is not straightforward. Each example is explained so that the implication for the statistics is very clear.

Some sociologists, notably Cohen and Young, have drawn our attention to the construction of moral panics by the media over a range of issues involving so-called deviant youth subcultures, drugs, football hooliganism etc. These have the effect of demonising youth in particular. Moral panics also put pressure on the authorities to police some groups more heavily, to sentence them more harshly and to introduce new laws to control and criminalise them. It is argued that such processes artificially amplify the OCS and tell us more about the moral anxieties of the media and what is newsworthy at any particular moment than about the nature of crime and criminality.

ℓ This candidate is systematically examining each influence on the statistics — in this case, media moral panics — and summarising that influence in some detail and with intelligent examples. There is a consistent focus on the question.

Interpretivists have spent a great deal of time and energy examining police culture and have concluded that the disproportionate presence of young people, working-class people and African-Caribbean people in the statistics may quite simply reflect police beliefs and stereotypes about these groups. Holdaway's research indicates that police organisational culture subscribes to negative stereotypes about black people which are reflected in derogatory jokes and language, and in the way that people from African-Caribbean backgrounds are treated in interaction with police officers. Moreover, a large number of ethnic-minority police officers are leaving the police because their fellow white officers have been racially abusive and hostile. The McPherson Report into the death of Stephen Lawrence in 2001 concluded that the London police were 'institutionally racist' — they were guilty of unwitting prejudice, ignorance, thoughtlessness and racial stereotyping which disadvantaged minority ethnic groups. Stop and search figures published in 2002 show that young blacks are five times more likely to be stopped by the police than young whites.

ℓ This is an excellent section which demonstrates a grasp of contemporary issues surrounding the impact of police culture on criminal statistics. Note how the first sentence addresses the question.

There is also evidence that the police may operate on the basis of stereotypes in regard to young, male and working-class offenders. Feminist sociologists argue that police occupational culture is patriarchal and dominated by a cult of masculinity which means that females are less likely to be stopped and arrested. It is a fact that females are more likely to be cautioned for the same types of crimes for which males are arrested. Such paternalism may result in female crime being seriously underestimated (although some feminists claim that women are quite simply less criminal than men).

e The analysis of police culture is rightly extended to include attitudes towards different genders. Again, note how the question is addressed.

Studies by sociologists such as Hood and Savage indicate similar possibilities operating in magistrates and crown courts. Judges and magistrates are recruited from narrow upper-middle-class and white backgrounds and may operate with unwitting prejudice towards working-class and black people in the courtroom when it comes to sentencing. Hood's study of crown courts in the West Midlands in the 1990s found that black youth were 17% more likely to be given custodial sentences compared with white youth for the same crime. Juries too may be operating on the basis of stereotypes rather than on the basis of objective facts. Experiments conducted at the London School of Economics found that juries were more willing to acquit white, smartly dressed, well-spoken men than people with working-class characteristics. This may be one reason why the middle classes are not heavily represented in the OCS. Interpretivists therefore conclude that the OCS may tell us more about judicial and jury biases than they tell us about criminality.

e Excellent knowledge and understanding are demonstrated in relation to magistrates, judges and juries and the analysis is focused accurately on how this affects the criminal statistics.

Marxists argue that the OCS give the impression that working-class people and black people are the main criminals in our society. However, Marxists are unhappy with this picture of crime. They believe that the OCS function as an ideological tool to criminalise the powerless and therefore justify repressive policing of them. There are essentially three reasons for this. First, the focus on working-class and black criminality diverts attention away from the criminal activities of the rich and powerful, i.e. white-collar and corporate crime — the financial value of which far exceeds that of street crime. Second, Box notes that the OCS criminalise those groups most likely to threaten the domination of the ruling class. Third, the statistics divide and rule sections of the working class — especially turning white against black, so weakening their revolutionary potential. Marxists therefore argue that the statistics tell us more about the capitalist class than they tell us about criminality.

e Perceptive and confident knowledge and understanding are demonstrated here. The candidate includes the phrase 'the statistics tell us more about' which indicates focused analysis and a recognition that the question needs to addressed consistently throughout.

Left realists are sceptical of these claims and accuse Marxists of romanticising working-class and black crime. They point out that victim surveys indicate real and justified fear of working-class and black crime in some urban areas. In other words, Lea and Young argue that the OCS are reliable and valid in their picture of

crime and criminality. Instead of dismissing crime as a social construction, as do both interpretivists and Marxists, Lea and Young argue that social policies should be tackling the relative deprivation, i.e. poverty, and perceived powerlessness that motivates young black and white working-class men to commit crime, mainly against their own ethnic group and social class.

e This is a focused evaluation of the Marxist perspective, although the interpretivist approach is slightly neglected. The candidate shows a confident grasp of left-realist concepts and theory.

Overall, then, the OCS do give us some insight into the groups involved in their collection, but despite amplification due to increased reporting, moral panics, policing and the neglect of white-collar crime, it is generally the case that working-class and black young males commit most crime. Instead of using the OCS to scapegoat and punish these groups, we should aim to address the inequalities that motivate such criminal behaviour.

e This is an intelligent and evaluative conclusion which addresses the question and makes an informed comment about where the future debate about the OCS might lead.

e It is difficult to see how an A2 candidate could improve upon this response. Despite a slight neglect of the interpretivist approach, this candidate more than compensates with a depth and grasp of other critiques of the OCS. The response contextualises the debate in terms of theoretical perspectives in a perceptive fashion, demonstrates a convincing grasp of a wide range of theories, studies and concepts and organises them in a logical and coherent way so that the question is addressed in almost every paragraph. The whole piece has an evaluative tone and the assessment of strengths and weaknesses is addressed in a sociologically focused and informed style. This candidate would therefore receive full marks across all three skill domains.

Overall mark: 60/60

Realist explanations of crime

Outline and assess the view that crime occurs because the benefits of crime outweigh the costs for the offender.

■ ■ ■

Answer to question 4: grade-A candidate

This view is associated with right realists such as Hirschi who believe that crime is a product of weak laws that fail to deter some social groups from committing crime. Other right realists such as Julius Wilson argue that most crime is opportunistic — we are all capable of committing crime but most of us are constrained by 'natural' social controls. In contrast, left realists argue that crime is a product of how people interpret their social and economic situation. The organisation of capitalist society penalises particular social groups and they experience both relative deprivation and powerlessness. Some respond to these feelings by turning to crime (although this is only one possible social reaction to their economic circumstances).

e The candidate clearly sets the theoretical scene of the debate by identifying the view contained in the essay title, i.e. right realism, and the alternative perspective, i.e. left realism.

Right realism subscribes to a very cynical view of human nature in that it suggests that human beings are naturally greedy, selfish and individualistic. Consequently, criminality is a natural outcome of human behaviour that needs constant control. Right realism rejects the notion that crime is caused by structural factors such as poverty. Wilson notes that if this were the case, crime rates would be much higher than they actually are, and argues that individual potential to commit crime has been kept in check by social controls traditionally put into place by family, education, the law and the community we live in. However, crime is increasing because such formal and informal controls are breaking down. Formal controls such as the law are failing because the emphasis has been on rehabilitation rather than on punishment and deterrence, with the consequence that criminals do not take the law seriously. Wilson argues that laws have got progressively weaker. Lawyers representing criminals now work the system for the benefit of their clients and laws are nowhere near tough enough. Moreover, Wilson and others argue that the police have lost their fight against crime — clear-up rates are poor and the criminal manipulation of the legal system means that offenders are soon back on the streets again committing crime. Right realism also argues that informal controls imposed by communities, i.e. by neighbours, friends and family, have broken down. Communities are in decline and, in particular, it is argued that the welfare state has undermined our sense of community responsibility.

question

e Excellent knowledge and understanding of how right realism sees the crime problem are demonstrated here.

Murray argues that we have seen a parallel rise in a social group he calls the underclass or new rabble. This lower-class subculture supposedly subscribes to a dependency culture and is uncommitted to conventional law-abiding values. Rather, its behaviour is the product of an immoral, criminal and deficient value system. It is workshy, dependent on welfare benefits, hostile to the law and lacking in any commitment to civilised society. These values and norms are transmitted from one generation to the next. Murray sees this underclass as primarily responsible for the rise in crime in recent years.

e This is a succinct summary of Murray's ideas on the underclass, demonstrating perceptive knowledge and understanding.

Hirschi brings all these ideas together in his 'control' theory. He notes that crime is the product of criminals making rational decisions after weighing up the risks of getting caught and the severity of punishment against the benefits of successfully committing crime. This costs-and-benefits approach prevents most of us committing crime because we have controls in our lives which mean that the costs of crime clearly outweigh the economic and personal benefits. Most people, according to Hirschi, have four key controls in their lives. First, they feel emotionally attached to their partners and families — involvement in crime may result in family breakdown and the threat of this is too great for most individuals. Second, most of us are committed to a career or business, having invested in education, and we have financial commitments such as mortgages and property. A criminal conviction would seriously undermine these. Third, people have reputations and statuses deriving from their involvement in their local communities which would be ruined by an accusation of criminality. Finally, people are normally socialised into a set of beliefs about discipline, rules and respect for others and the law. This deters most of us from committing crime. Hirschi therefore suggests that attachment, commitment, involvement and belief act as profound checks on behaviour and prevent the majority of us from committing crime.

e The candidate focuses on the central element of the essay in a perceptive, analytical and convincing fashion.

Hirschi goes on to point out that some social groups are likely to lack these controls. Young people, for example, have not yet committed themselves to a career, a family, financial investments and adult reputations and so are less constrained by these factors. Murray argues that the underclass lacks these controls too. Membership of this group does not involve subscribing to conventional controls — rather, it involves a rejection of them.

e Excellent interpretation and analysis skills are demonstrated in this paragraph as the candidate applies Hirschi's theories to the young and the underclass.

Right realists believe that the best way to decrease crime is to take practical measures to reduce opportunities to commit crime and to make life more difficult for the criminal. The costs of crime must clearly outweigh the benefits in terms of certainty of capture and heavy punishment. Wilson strongly recommended 'zero tolerance' — saturating urban areas with a heavy police presence and not tolerating any infringement of the law. The 'three strikes and you're out' policy adopted by some US states advocates putting people in prison for long periods after a third offence no matter how trivial it is. The Labour government's recent commitment to cracking down on the parents of delinquent children and on a range of antisocial behaviour is a reflection of this type of right-realist thinking. Labour is also suggesting that the general public needs to make crime more difficult by investing in more security and surveillance. This is known as target hardening or designing out crime.

e The candidate demonstrates good contemporary knowledge and understanding of right-realist solutions to crime, as well as perceptive interpretation of current social policy.

A number of critiques of this right-realist position have developed in recent years. First, right realism does tend to subscribe to an uncritical acceptance of the reliability and validity of the official criminal statistics. There is no sense that these might be a social construction, i.e. a product of increased reporting, new counting procedures, police discretion and stereotyping etc. Second, Marxists are critical of right-realist views of human nature. They argue that criminal behaviour is the product of a capitalist culture that encourages competition, individualism and greed. Third, neo-Weberian thinkers argue that there is no evidence that an underclass with a value system distinct from that of mainstream society actually exists. They argue instead that some sections of the working class have experienced poverty because of economic and social influences beyond their control. For example, globalisation has led to economic recession in some parts of the UK as employers move their operations to less developed societies with cheaper overheads. Such poverty has led to the emergence of an economic underclass characterised by high involuntary unemployment rather than being workshy. Moreover, members of this underclass are not happy about welfare dependency — surveys indicate that they would much rather work and earn a wage. It is argued that theories such as Murray's end up scapegoating the poor and contributing to the view that they somehow deserve more surveillance and controls. This fulfils the prophecy that the working class is more criminal, and drives up the statistics for working-class crime.

e The candidate identifies three substantive criticisms of right realism and supports these using conceptually confident illustration. However, evaluation would have benefited from some reference to the strengths of right realism.

Left realists argue that right-realist policies reinforce social and economic inequalities even further because only the middle classes can really afford to protect

question

themselves from crime. Designing out crime may result in middle-class fortress enclaves protected by security guards and cameras. This is likely to increase the already heavy victimisation of the working-class and ethnic minorities who live in inner-city areas.

e The candidate uses a left-realist critique of right realism as a springboard to examine this alternative approach to law and order.

Left realists like Young and Lea generally agree that the official criminal statistics can be distorted by police stereotyping etc., but they conclude that despite these influences, groups such as young working-class and black males do commit more crime than other groups. This observation has been backed up by surveys such as the Islington Crime Survey, which also notes that most of the victims of street crime committed by these groups tend to be working class and black. Left realists reject the right-realist view that most crime is opportunistic and evolves from a lack of controls and weak laws or that a criminal underclass has emerged. Instead, they argue that crime is a product of the way modern societies are organised. Like Merton and Marxists such as Gordon, they argue that some social groups — the working class and young blacks — are denied the same opportunities as the rest of the population with regard to careers, living standards and acquisition of consumer goods. Such groups compare themselves with their middle-class or white peers and feel relatively deprived. They also feel marginalised, i.e. that society has little interest in them or even that society is deliberately holding them back, e.g. through racist policies and policing. They feel powerless to change their situation and are consequently frustrated. Young and Lea argue that most people in this position actually conform by channelling their frustration into legitimate subcultural outlets such as religion, sport and music. Some, however, will turn to criminal or delinquent subcultures which operate in the 'black economy'. Sometimes such frustration erupts in urban disorder and riots.

e The candidate demonstrates excellent knowledge and understanding of left realism whilst continuing to evaluate aspects of right realism.

Left realism is essentially a magpie theory which has borrowed imaginatively from both Mertonian anomie theory and Marxism to combine the influences of structure and interpretation in the view that crime is the result of how people interpret their structural position. However, the left realists have done no empirical research into the motives of criminals in order to check the validity of this view. Moreover, their theory tends to emphasise street crime such as mugging and robbery at the expense of other important types of crime. Nevertheless, the theory can be applauded for getting to grips with an unpleasant and politically unpopular fact — that working-class people and black people are more potentially criminal than other social groups, that their victims are also working class and black and that we need to understand and address the motives behind criminality and how these are related to the social organisation of the societies we live in if we are to tackle crime successfully.

e This is evaluation which focuses on both the strengths and weaknesses of left realism in a convincing fashion.

Overall, left realists are critical of the right-realist idea that crime results when the benefits of crime outweigh the costs and the risks. However, it may be the case that the economically deprived and the powerless identified by Young and Lea have got less to lose in terms of commitments than more affluent groups. The decision to commit crime may be a product of economic desperation rather than commitment to a deviant culture.

e Although this evaluative conclusion is a little simplistic, it demonstrates some thought as to how these opposing approaches to crime might be reconciled.

e This essay reveals a wide-ranging and detailed knowledge and understanding of both realist theories and the concepts and evidence that underpin them. The candidate deals confidently with interrelated concepts and articulates them clearly, and would score 28/28 marks for knowledge and understanding. The material selected is relevant and is organised in such a way that it always focuses on analysing the central premise of the question set. Consequently, the candidate would receive the full 16 marks for interpretation and analysis. Evaluation is detailed and well developed but is slightly unbalanced in that it focuses mainly on weaknesses and pays relatively little attention to strengths. The candidate would therefore receive 14/16 for this skill.

Overall mark: 58/60

uestion **5**

Gender and crime

Outline and assess the view that women are more likely to be the victims of crime than to be offenders.

■ ■ ■

Task

This question is for you to try yourself. You should spend some time researching suitable material and making notes, and then try to write the answer in 60 minutes — the time you will be allowed in the examination. Below are a few pointers to help you get on the right track.

Your **introduction** should set the scene in two ways:
- What do the official criminal statistics tell us about the volume of female crime and the types of crime being committed by women in comparison with men?
- What are the social assumptions generally made about women as victims?

How should this essay **develop**?
- Start by evaluating the view of women offenders found in the official criminal statistics, i.e. why might this picture of female criminality not be accurate? Examine studies of police culture and especially the chivalry factor, the use of cautions and the role of the courts. Studies might include Heidensohn, Campbell, Carlen and Worrall.
- You are likely to conclude that women commit less crime than men. You therefore need to explain why women are less likely to be offenders by examining in turn and in detail:
  — the role of gender role socialisation and especially the values, roles and social controls associated with masculinity/femininity
  — the male dominance of public space and employment etc.
- Examine the reasons why women do commit crime: poverty, response to domestic violence, excitement and image, girl gangs.

Examine **the alternative view** in the essay title about women being more likely to be victims.
- What do sociological studies tell us about women as victims?
  — studies of domestic violence, e.g. Stanko
  — studies of sexual crime, e.g. Lees
  — victim studies such as Hanmer and Saunders, and the Islington Crime Survey

A possible **conclusion** could read as follows:
Despite the recent rise in female violence and even allowing for the unreliability of the criminal statistics because of paternalistic policing and judicial practices, women do not commit as much crime as men. The key explanation may lie in gender role socialisation. However, it is important to note that young men are more at risk of being victims of crime than women of all age groups, although women's fear of crime in inner-city areas is not unrealistic.

Ethnicity and crime

Outline and assess the view that ethnic-minority crime is the product of relative deprivation and powerlessness.

■ ■ ■

Task

This question is for you to try yourself. You should spend some time researching suitable material and making notes, and then try to write the answer in 60 minutes — the time you will be allowed in the examination. Below are a few pointers to help you get on the right track.

Your **introduction** should set the scene for this debate in two ways.
- Define your terms. What is meant by 'ethnic-minority crime'? Do you intend to focus on a range of ethnic-minority groups or the one which dominates the official criminal statistics, i.e. African-Caribbeans?
- Identify the view contained in the title (i.e. left realism) and briefly outline the theory of crime it represents. Briefly contrast it with alternative views such as Gilroy's take on neo-Marxism or Cashmore's blocked-opportunity theory.

How should this essay **develop**?
- Outline what the criminal statistics tell us about ethnic-minority crime.
- Evaluate this official view of ethnic-minority crime by examining police practices (Holdaway's work on police culture and the McPherson Report are useful sources here) and judicial processes (e.g. Hood).
- What is the left-realist view of the ethnic-minority presence in the official criminal statistics?

The **focus on the left-realist view** should include:
- how ethnic-minority crime was perceived by the Islington Crime Survey
- a clear explanation of the three interrelated components of Young and Lea's theory, i.e. 'relative deprivation', 'marginalisation' and 'subcultural responses', with illustrations/examples

The **evaluation of the left-realist view** should focus on:
- the strengths of the theory, i.e. its realistic approach to unpopular facts about who commits crime, the voice it gives to victims of crime and its work on intra-ethnic crime
- specific weaknesses, i.e. the lack of empirical research and the overemphasis on street crime

Discussion of **alternative theories** might include:
- Cashmore's anomie/blocked-opportunity theory — note the resemblance to left realism

question

- Murray's underclass theory — possibly link to Hirschi — do African-Caribbean youth have fewer community controls, commitments etc?
- Gilroy's ideas about black crime being a political response to interpretations of historical experience (slavery and colonialism) and present-day racism

The **conclusion** could focus on why African-Caribbeans commit more crime today than in the past or why different ethnic-minority groups experience different crime rates.